BOSTON

TRAVEL GUIDE 2023

Exploring Boston like a Local: A Comprehensive Travel Guide and Essential Tips. Insider Secrets, Local Favorites, and Off-the-Beaten-Path Experiences.

Copyright © 2023 Matt Dean. All rights reserved.

Thankful to you for consenting to protected innovation guidelines by downloading this book through genuine methods and by not replicating, checking, or spreading any piece of this book.

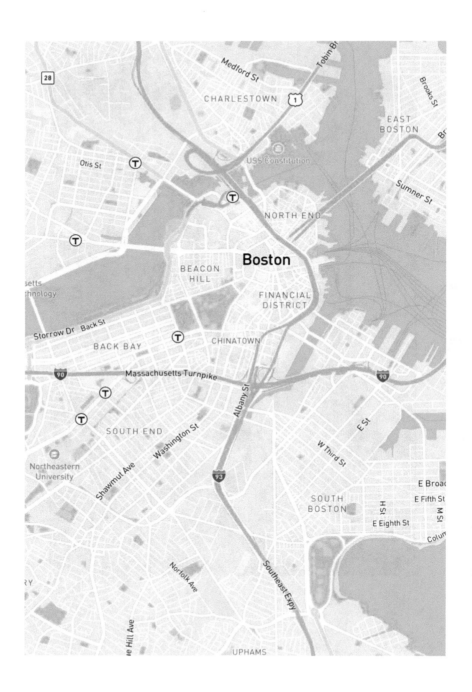

4

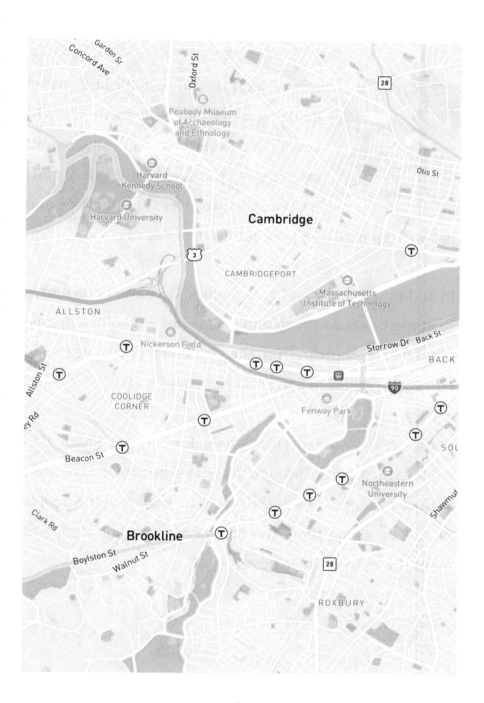

About Author

Matt Hood is an established travel guidebook author, with more than 10 years of experience in the travel industry. A passionate traveller, Matt has travelled to over 30 countries and has written extensively about his experiences.

In addition to his travel guidebooks, Matt also contributes to numerous travel blogs and magazines. He holds a degree in travel and tourism from the University of Michigan and currently resides in San Francisco, California.

Matt Hood is the perfect guide for anyone looking to explore the world. Through his books, he provides readers with an insider's view of the places he visits and the people he meets, giving them the confidence and knowledge to make the most of their travels.

TABLE OF CONTENTS

WELCOME TO BOSTON

Welcome to Boston, I'm Matt Hood, your trusted travel guidebook author, and I'm thrilled to take you on an unforgettable journey through the vibrant city of Boston. Whether you're a history buff, a food lover, a culture enthusiast, or simply an explorer at heart, this comprehensive guide is designed to cater to all your travel desires.

Allow me to introduce myself and share why this book should be your go-to resource for discovering the best of Boston. With over a decade of experience in the travel industry, I've had the privilege of exploring countless cities around the world. However, it is Boston that has captured my heart and inspired me to share its wonders with you. Having extensively researched, explored, and lived in Boston, I've gained a deep understanding of its rich history, diverse neighbourhoods, and hidden gems.

Now, let's talk about what makes this travel guide special. This book is not just a collection of facts and recommendations; it's a carefully curated companion that will accompany you on your Boston adventure. Packed with insider tips, detailed maps, stunning photography, and engaging narratives, This Travel guide ensures that you experience the city like a true local. From iconic landmarks like the Freedom Trail and Fenway Park to hidden gems in neighbourhoods like Beacon Hill and the North End, this guide covers it all.

One of the highlights of this book is the inclusion of a One-week Itinerary in Boston, which is perfect for first-time visitors or those looking to make the most of their limited time. This meticulously planned itinerary takes you through the city's must-see attractions, iconic landmarks, cultural hotspots, and mouthwatering dining experiences. Follow the itinerary, and you'll be able to immerse yourself in the essence of Boston while making lifelong memories.

But that's not all! I understand that exploring beyond Boston is equally enticing, which is why I've included an Itinerary Beyond Boston. you'll find exciting day trips and regional adventures that allow you to discover the beauty of New England. From the historic towns of Salem and Lexington to the picturesque Cape Cod and Martha's Vineyard, these destinations offer a perfect blend of history, nature, and coastal charm.

As your trusted travel companion, I also provide practical information, such as accommodation options, dining recommendations, and transportation tips. Whether you're seeking luxury, mid-range, or budget-friendly hotels, the guidebook has got you covered. Additionally, I've handpicked the best restaurants, bars, and shopping spots, ensuring you have a memorable culinary and retail experience.

Finally, I want to express my sincere gratitude to all the readers who have supported my previous travel guidebooks. It is your trust and encouragement that inspire me to continue exploring and sharing the wonders of the world. I have poured my passion for travel and love for Boston into every page of this book, and I hope it becomes your ultimate companion on your journey through this remarkable city.

So, without further ado, get ready to uncover the hidden treasures, embrace the fascinating history, indulge in delectable cuisine, and create unforgettable memories in Boston. Let this Ultimate Travel Guide be your ticket to an extraordinary adventure in the heart of New England.

Bon voyage!

Matt Hood

CHAPTER 1

INTRODUCTION

Overview of Boston

Welcome to Boston, where the past intertwines with the present, inviting you to embark on an extraordinary journey through time.

Boston is the vibrant capital city of Massachusetts! Known for its rich history, cultural diversity, and iconic landmarks, Boston offers an unforgettable travel experience that will leave you captivated. In this introduction, we will delve into the fascinating history of Boston, what to expect during your stay, and the unique people and culture that make this city truly special.

Boston's history is deeply rooted in the founding of the United States. As one of the oldest cities in the country, Boston played a pivotal role in the American Revolution, with events such as the Boston Tea Party and the Battle of Bunker Hill shaping the nation's history. Walking through the city's cobblestone streets and historic neighbourhoods is like stepping back in time, where the echoes of the past blend seamlessly with the vibrancy of the present.

Today, Boston stands as a bustling metropolis that effortlessly blends its rich heritage with modernity. From the architectural grandeur of the Massachusetts State House to the cobblestone lanes of Beacon Hill, the city's landmarks tell stories of a bygone era. Boston Common, the oldest public park in the country, offers a serene oasis amidst the bustling cityscape, while the vibrant waterfront showcases the city's maritime heritage.

When visiting Boston, you can expect a diverse range of experiences that cater to all interests. The city's renowned educational institutions, including Harvard University and MIT, attract scholars and intellectuals from around the world, contributing to a vibrant intellectual and cultural scene. Boston's museums, such as the Museum of Fine Arts and the Isabella Stewart Gardner Museum, house world-class art collections that will inspire and captivate art enthusiasts.

As you explore Boston, you'll encounter a city that celebrates its cultural diversity. From the historic Italian district of the North End, where the aroma of freshly baked cannoli fills the air, to the vibrant Chinatown with its bustling markets and authentic cuisine, Boston's neighbourhoods offer a culinary journey like no other. The city's Irish heritage is celebrated during the annual St. Patrick's Day parade, while the Boston Pops Orchestra captivates audiences with its renowned performances.

The people of Boston, known as Bostonians, are known for their warmth, resilience, and a strong sense of community. As a city that cherishes its sports teams, such as the Red Sox and the Celtics, you'll witness firsthand the passion and pride that Bostonians have for their home teams. Engaging in conversation with locals will reveal their deep knowledge of the city's history and their unwavering love for their beloved "Beantown."

As you embark on your journey through Boston, prepare to be immersed in its rich history, iconic landmarks, and vibrant culture. From exploring the Freedom Trail, a 2.5-mile route that takes you through significant Revolutionary War sites, to indulging in the city's delectable seafood and experiencing its thriving arts scene, Boston offers a multitude of experiences that will leave a lasting impression.

History of Boston

Boston is a place where history comes alive. Steeped in centuries of stories, this iconic city played a pivotal role in the birth of the United States and continues to be a vibrant hub of cultural, educational, and economic significance. As we explore the overview of Boston, we delve into its captivating history, from its humble beginnings to its rise as a centre of innovation and intellectual prowess.

The story of Boston begins in the early 17th century when English Puritans settled in the area known as Shawmut Peninsula. Led by John Winthrop, they established a community and named it Boston, after the town in Lincolnshire, England. The settlers faced many challenges, including harsh winters, but their determination and resilience laid the foundation for the city's growth.

During the 18th century, Boston became a hotbed of revolutionary fervour. It was in this city that the seeds of American independence were sown. The Stamp Act protests, the Boston Tea Party, and the Battles of

Lexington and Concord ignited the flames of revolution. Bostonians stood at the forefront of the fight against British oppression, and their spirit would shape the course of American history.

One of the most iconic symbols of Boston's revolutionary legacy is the Freedom Trail. This 2.5-mile historic trail winds through the city, connecting 16 significant sites that played a role in the American Revolution. Walking along the red-brick path, visitors can immerse themselves in the history and stories of courageous patriots who fought for liberty and freedom.

Boston's role as a centre of education and intellectual pursuits began to flourish in the early 19th century. The city became home to prestigious universities, such as Harvard and MIT, cementing its reputation as an intellectual powerhouse. Scholars, philosophers, and innovators flocked to Boston, contributing to its rich academic and cultural landscape.

The city's growth continued into the 19th and 20th centuries, fueled by industrialization and waves of immigrants seeking better opportunities. Irish, Italian, Jewish, and other communities added to the vibrant tapestry of Boston's cultural diversity. Neighbourhoods like the North End, known for its Italian heritage, and Beacon Hill, with its well-preserved 19th-century architecture, reflect the city's immigrant history and offer glimpses into the past.

Boston's history is intricately linked to the sea, and its waterfront played a crucial role in its development. As a bustling port, Boston saw trade and commerce flourish, connecting it to other parts of the world. The waterfront is still a vibrant area today, with attractions like the New England Aquarium and the scenic Harborwalk, offering stunning views of the city skyline.

The rich history of Boston is beautifully preserved in its architecture and landmarks. The Massachusetts State House, with its iconic golden dome, stands as a symbol of the city's political heritage. Faneuil Hall, a historic marketplace and meeting hall, once hosted revolutionary speeches and continues to be a vibrant centre for commerce and culture.

To truly understand Boston's history, a visit to the renowned museums is a must. The Museum of Fine Arts houses an extensive collection of art spanning different eras and cultures, while the Boston Tea Party Ships & Museum offers an immersive experience of the events that led to the American Revolution. The Paul Revere House, a preserved 17th-century home, provides a glimpse into the life of this famous patriot.

The city's story is deeply intertwined with the birth and growth of a nation. Boston's indomitable spirit, intellectual legacy, and commitment to preserving its historical heritage make it a captivating destination for history enthusiasts, scholars, and curious travellers alike.

Geography and Climate

Boston is nestled in the eastern part of Massachusetts, along the beautiful coast of the Atlantic Ocean. The city's unique geography is characterized by a captivating blend of waterfront charm and rolling hills that create a stunning backdrop for your Boston adventure.

Boston Harbor, with its sparkling waters, is an integral part of the city's identity. Stretching along Massachusetts Bay, it offers a picturesque setting for boat cruises, water sports, and strolls along the harbour walk. Exploring the harbour and its islands allows you to escape the urban pace and immerse yourself in the tranquillity of the sea.

The topography of Boston is defined by gentle hills, verdant parks, and serene lakes. The city is surrounded by inviting green spaces that beckon outdoor enthusiasts to explore. Among these natural treasures is the renowned Arnold Arboretum, a sprawling botanical garden showcasing a diverse collection of trees and plants. The

Arnold Arboretum is a haven for nature lovers, providing a peaceful sanctuary within the bustling city.

Boston's climate exhibits a temperate maritime pattern, with distinct seasons that each bring their allure and activities. Summers in Boston are typically mild and warm, with temperatures ranging from 15 to 25 degrees Celsius (59 to 77 degrees Fahrenheit). The longer daylight hours create a vibrant atmosphere, enticing locals and visitors to revel in outdoor dining, picnics in the parks, and leisurely walks along the Charles River Esplanade.

Autumn in Boston paints the city with a stunning display of colours as the foliage transforms into a tapestry of vibrant hues. Temperatures begin to cool, ranging from 5 to 15 degrees Celsius (41 to 59 degrees Fahrenheit), providing the perfect weather for exploring the city's historic neighbourhoods and meandering through the Boston Common. Fall is also a time of festive celebrations, with the city coming alive during events like the Boston Harborfest and Head of the Charles Regatta.

Winter in Boston blankets the city with a picturesque layer of snow, creating a magical ambience. Temperatures during this season range from -6 to 3 degrees Celsius (21 to 37 degrees Fahrenheit). Embrace the winter wonderland and indulge in activities such as ice skating on the Boston Common Frog Pond or witnessing the iconic Boston Christmas tree lighting at the Prudential Center. Boston's rich cultural scene thrives even during the colder months, with theatre performances, museum exhibits, and cosy cafes welcoming visitors.

Spring marks the rejuvenation of Boston as nature awakens from its winter slumber. Temperatures gradually rise, ranging from 5 to 15 degrees Celsius (41 to 59 degrees Fahrenheit), bringing a burst of colour and new life to the city. Embrace the blooming flowers and budding trees as you explore the renowned Public Garden or take a stroll along the Harborwalk. Spring is the perfect time to witness the Boston Marathon, a legendary race that embodies the city's resilience and spirit.

No matter the season, Boston's unique blend of coastal beauty, rolling hills, and vibrant cultural scene ensures that there is always something captivating to discover. So, prepare to embark on a journey through the seasons and experience the ever-changing allure of this remarkable city.

By Air:

Boston is a major transportation hub with a well-connected international airport, offering convenient access to the city for travellers from around the world. Logan International Airport (BOS) is Boston's primary airport and one of the busiest airports in the United States. Here's everything you need to know about reaching Boston by air:

Logan International Airport (BOS):

Located in East Boston, approximately 4 miles from downtown Boston, Logan International Airport serves as the main gateway to the city.

The airport offers a wide range of domestic and international flights, with direct connections to major cities throughout the United States, Europe, Canada, and other destinations.

To plan your trip effectively, it is recommended to visit the official website of Logan International Airport (www.massport.com/logan-airport) for detailed information on flight schedules, airlines operating at the airport, facilities, services, and other useful traveller resources. Checking the website before your journey will ensure you have the most up-to-date information.

Transportation from Logan International Airport to the City Center:

- Taxi: Taxis are readily available outside the airport terminals, providing a convenient and direct means of transportation to the city centre. The travel time can vary depending on traffic conditions, typically ranging from 20 to 30 minutes. The fare will depend on the time of day and the exact destination within the city.
- Airport Shuttle: Several shuttle services operate between Logan International Airport and downtown Boston, as well as various hotels in the area. These shuttles offer a cost-effective option, with fixed rates and scheduled departures.

- Public Transportation: The Massachusetts Bay Transportation Authority (MBTA) operates the Silver Line SL1 bus service, which connects the airport terminals with various subway stations in downtown Boston. From there, you can easily access other parts of the city using the subway system, known as the "T." The subway provides a convenient and affordable transportation option for travellers.

- Ride-Sharing Services: Ride-sharing services like Uber and Lyft are also available at Logan International Airport, providing an alternative and convenient way to reach your destination in Boston. The designated pickup areas can be found outside the terminals.

By Land

Boston is well-connected by road and rail, making it easily accessible for travellers arriving from neighbouring cities and states. Here are some options to consider:

Road: Boston is connected to the interstate highway system, allowing for easy access by car from various locations. Interstate 90 (I-90), also known as the Massachusetts Turnpike, is a major highway that connects Boston with cities such as New York, Chicago, and other destinations across the country. Additionally, Interstate 95 (I-95) runs along the East Coast and provides access to Boston from neighbouring states.

Train: Amtrak, the national rail service in the United States, operates train routes that connect Boston with other major cities along the East Coast, including New York, Washington, D.C., and Philadelphia. The historic South Station serves as the primary train station in Boston, offering convenient access to the city centre and other destinations.

By Sea:

While Boston is a coastal city, direct sea routes for reaching the city are limited. However, Boston is a popular port of call for cruise ships travelling along the East Coast. Passengers on these cruises have the opportunity to explore the city for a day as part of their itinerary.

Getting Around Boston

Boston offers a range of transportation options to help visitors explore its attractions and navigate the city efficiently. Here's a comprehensive guide on getting around Boston:

Public Transportation: Boston has a well-developed public transportation system, operated by the Massachusetts Bay Transportation Authority (MBTA) or "the T." The T consists of subway lines, buses, and commuter trains, providing convenient access to various parts of the city. Here are some key points to know about travelling by public transportation in Boston:

Subway (the T): The subway, known as the "T," is a popular and efficient way to get around Boston. It consists of four lines: Red, Orange, Blue, and Green. The subway operates from early morning until midnight, with extended hours on weekends and during special events. Fare prices depend on the distance travelled, and tickets can be purchased at automated vending machines located in the subway stations.

Buses: The MBTA operates an extensive bus network that covers the entire city, including neighbourhoods and suburbs. Buses generally operate from early morning until midnight, with reduced frequency during late evenings and early mornings. Bus stops are marked throughout the city, and electronic displays at the stops provide real-time information about bus arrivals and schedules. Fare prices are the same as those for the subway.

Commuter Trains: For travellers venturing outside of Boston, commuter trains provide convenient connections to suburbs and nearby towns. The commuter rail lines operate from Boston's North Station and South Station, offering access to destinations such as Salem, Cambridge, and Worcester. Fare prices vary based on the distance travelled.

Taxi and Ride-Sharing Services: Taxi and ride-sharing services like Uber and Lyft are widely available in Boston. Taxis can be hailed on the street or found at designated taxi stands throughout the city. Ride-sharing services can be accessed through mobile apps. Both options provide convenient door-to-door transportation, but fares may vary depending on demand, time of day, and distance travelled.

Biking: Boston is a bike-friendly city with an extensive network of bike lanes and paths. Biking can be a convenient and enjoyable way to explore the city's attractions. Visitors can rent bicycles from various bike-sharing programs available, such as Bluebikes, which provides easy access to bikes at stations located throughout the city. Safety regulations, including wearing helmets, are strongly recommended when cycling in Boston.

Walking: Boston is a compact and walkable city, particularly in its historic neighbourhoods and downtown areas. Many popular attractions, such as the Freedom

Trail, Beacon Hill, and the Public Garden, are within walking distance of each other. Exploring on foot allows visitors to immerse themselves in Boston's vibrant streetscapes, historic sites, and charming architecture.

Car Rental: While having a car is not necessary for exploring Boston's city centre, renting a car can be useful for day trips or for those who prefer the flexibility of having their vehicle. Rental car agencies can be found at the airport and throughout the city. However, it's important to note that Boston's narrow streets, heavy traffic, and limited parking can make driving in the city challenging. Additionally, parking fees can be quite expensive, especially in central areas.

CHAPTER 2

EXPLORING BOSTON: BACK BAY

Copley Square

Copley Square is a vibrant and historic public square located in the Back Bay neighbourhood of Boston. This iconic square is surrounded by architectural gems, and renowned cultural institutions, and serves as a hub for shopping, dining, and entertainment. With its rich history and central location, Copley Square is a must-visit destination for travellers looking to experience the heart of Boston.

Why Go:

Copley Square offers a blend of history, culture, and contemporary city life. Visitors can admire the stunning architecture of landmarks such as Trinity Church and the

Boston Public Library, immerse themselves in the art exhibitions at the Museum of Fine Arts, and indulge in the vibrant shopping scene along Newbury Street. The square also hosts various events and festivals throughout the year, providing a lively and engaging atmosphere for both locals and visitors.

When to Go:

Copley Square is enjoyable to explore year-round, with each season offering its unique charm. Spring and fall are particularly delightful, as the weather is mild, and the surrounding foliage creates a picturesque backdrop. Summer brings bustling energy to the square, with outdoor cafes and street performers entertaining visitors. Winter transforms Copley Square into a winter wonderland, adorned with holiday decorations and hosting festive events.

Outdoor Activities

Boston Public Garden:

Spring and summer are ideal for strolling through the beautiful gardens, enjoying the blooming flowers, and taking a relaxing boat ride on the pond.

Charles River Esplanade:

Summer and early fall provide the perfect weather for walking, jogging, or biking along the scenic paths of the Esplanade. Visitors can also rent a kayak or paddleboard to enjoy the river.

Freedom Trail:

The Freedom Trail showcases Boston's revolutionary history, including sites like the Massachusetts State House and Paul Revere's House.

Newbury Street is a vibrant and iconic destination located in the heart of Boston's Back Bay neighbourhood. This historic street is renowned for its charming brownstone buildings, upscale shops, trendy boutiques, art galleries, and a thriving culinary scene. With its unique blend of history, culture, and fashion, Newbury Street is a must-visit for travellers looking to indulge in a quintessential Boston experience.

Why Go:

Newbury Street offers a captivating atmosphere where visitors can immerse themselves in a blend of high-end shopping, art appreciation, and delectable dining. The street's charming architecture, lined with picturesque tree-lined sidewalks, creates a delightful ambience for strolls and exploration. Whether you're seeking the latest fashion trends, local art, or a memorable dining experience, Newbury Street provides a one-of-a-kind destination for a truly Bostonian experience.

When to Go:

Newbury Street is bustling year-round, each season offering its unique charm. Spring and fall are particularly delightful, as the mild weather allows for comfortable shopping and outdoor dining experiences. Summer brings vibrant energy with outdoor festivals and street performances. Winter transforms Newbury Street into a winter wonderland, adorned with holiday decorations and cosy storefronts.

Outdoor Activities:

Copley Square:

Anytime during the year, but spring and fall offer comfortable temperatures for exploring the square's iconic landmarks, visiting art exhibitions, and enjoying the bustling atmosphere.

Prudential Center, commonly known as "The Pru," is a renowned shopping and dining destination located in the Back Bay neighbourhood of Boston. This iconic complex features a mix of high-end retailers, delicious eateries, and stunning views from its observation deck. With its central location and diverse offerings, Prudential Center is a must-visit for both locals and visitors seeking a memorable Boston experience.

Why Go:

Prudential Center offers a dynamic atmosphere where visitors can indulge in world-class shopping, savour diverse culinary delights, and enjoy panoramic views of the city. Whether you're a fashion enthusiast, a food lover, or simply seeking a vibrant urban setting, The Pru provides an all-encompassing experience in the heart of Boston.

When to Go:

Prudential Center welcomes visitors year-round, each season offering its unique charm. Spring and fall are particularly pleasant, with mild temperatures ideal for exploring the outdoor spaces and enjoying rooftop dining. Summer brings a lively atmosphere with outdoor events and concerts, while the holiday season adds a festive touch with beautiful decorations and seasonal activities.

Outdoor Activities:

Prudential Skywalk Observatory:

Ascend to the top of the Prudential Tower and enjoy panoramic views of Boston and beyond. The Skywalk Observatory offers a 360-degree vantage point, providing breathtaking vistas of the city's skyline, landmarks, and harbour.

The Shops at Prudential Center:

Embark on a retail therapy adventure through The Shops at Prudential Center. Discover a diverse collection of upscale boutiques, designer stores, and speciality shops offering fashion, accessories, home goods, and more.

Prudential Center Garden:

Take a moment to relax and appreciate the beauty of the Prudential Center Garden. This tranquil oasis amidst the bustling city features lush greenery, colourful flowers, and comfortable seating areas, providing a peaceful retreat.

The Boston Public Library (BPL) is a historic and culturally significant landmark located in Copley Square. Established in 1848, it is one of the oldest public libraries in the United States and serves as a repository of knowledge and a hub of intellectual activity. The library's grand architecture, extensive collections, and engaging exhibitions make it a must-visit destination for literature enthusiasts, history buffs, and anyone seeking a glimpse into Boston's rich literary heritage.

Why Go:

The Boston Public Library offers a unique opportunity to explore a treasure trove of books, manuscripts, artwork, and historical artefacts. It provides a serene and inspiring environment for reading, research, and contemplation. Beyond its literary offerings, the library hosts engaging events, lectures, and exhibitions that showcase the city's vibrant cultural scene. Whether you're a book lover, a history enthusiast, or simply seeking a tranquil space to unwind, the BPL is a haven of knowledge and inspiration.

When to Go:

The Boston Public Library welcomes visitors year-round, and each season brings its charm. Spring and fall offer pleasant weather, making it ideal for exploring the library's outdoor spaces and strolling through nearby Copley Square. Winter provides a cosy atmosphere, perfect for immersing yourself in the library's vast collection. It's advisable to check the library's website for specific opening hours and any special exhibitions or events happening during your visit.

Outdoor Activities:

Freedom Trail:

Embark on a historic journey by following the Freedom Trail, a 2.5-mile route that showcases Boston's revolutionary history. The trail passes through significant sites such as the Massachusetts State House, Paul Revere's House, and the Old North Church, offering a glimpse into the city's past.

Best Places to Stay @ Back Bay

The Fairmont Copley Plaza:

- Address: 138 St James Ave, Boston, MA 02116
- Phone: +1 617-267-5300
- Website:www.fairmont.com/copley-plaza-Boston

A luxurious and historic hotel offering elegant rooms, exceptional service, and a prime location near Copley Square. Guests can enjoy a fitness centre, on-site dining options, and easy access to Boston's top attractions.

The Lenox Hotel:

- Address: 61 Exeter St, Boston, MA 02116
- Phone: +1 617-536-5300
- Website: www.lenoxhotel.com

A boutique hotel is known for its timeless charm and personalized service. Located steps away from Copley Square, the hotel features comfortable rooms, a rooftop terrace, and an award-winning restaurant.

The Eliot Hotel:

- Address: 370 Commonwealth Ave, Boston, MA 02215
- Phone: +1 617-267-1607
- Website: www.eliothotel.com

A luxurious boutique hotel offering elegant rooms, attentive service, and a prime location near Newbury Street. The hotel boasts a stylish atmosphere, a renowned French restaurant, and amenities designed for a comfortable stay.

The Colonnade Hotel:

- Address: 120 Huntington Ave, Boston, MA 02116
- Phone: +1 617-424-7000
- Website: www.colonnadehotel.com

A stylish and luxurious hotel situated near Prudential Center. The Colonnade Hotel features elegant rooms, a rooftop pool, a rooftop lounge with breathtaking views, and a variety of dining options within walking distance.

Hilton Boston Back Bay:

- Address: 40 Dalton St, Boston, MA 02115
- Phone: +1 617-236-1100
- Website: www.hiltonbackbay.com

Located steps away from Prudential Center, this Hilton hotel offers comfortable accommodations, a fitness centre, and a restaurant. With its convenient location and excellent amenities, it provides a pleasant stay for travellers exploring the area.

The Westin Copley Place:

- Address: 10 Huntington Ave, Boston, MA 02116

- Phone: +1 617-262-9600

- Website:www.marriott.com/hotels/travel/boswi-the-westin-copley-place-boston

Situated in the Back Bay neighbourhood, The Westin Copley Place offers comfortable accommodations, a rooftop pool, a fitness centre, and several dining options. Enjoy the convenience of being close to the library, shopping, and other attractions while enjoying a relaxing stay.

Stephanie's On Newbury:

- Address: 190 Newbury St, Boston, MA 02116
- Phone: +1 617-236-0990
- Website: www.stephaniesonnewbury.com
- Hours: Monday-Sunday 8:00 AM - 9:00 PM

Description: A popular restaurant offering American comfort food with a contemporary twist. Stephanie's On Newbury is known for its relaxed atmosphere, delicious brunch options, and outdoor seating perfect for people-watching.

Ostra:

- Address: 1 Charles St S, Boston, MA 02116
- Phone: +1 617-421-1200
- Website: www.ostraboston.com
- Hours: Monday-Sunday 4:00 PM - 10:00 PM

Description: A sophisticated seafood restaurant offering a refined dining experience. Ostra serves fresh, globally-inspired dishes, and exquisite cocktails, and features an extensive wine list.

Sonsie:

- Address: 327 Newbury St, Boston, MA 02115
- Phone: +1 617-351-2500
- Website: www.sonsieboston.com
- Hours: Monday-Sunday 10:00 AM - 11:00 PM

A lively bistro offering a diverse menu featuring American and international dishes. Sonsie is known for its vibrant atmosphere, sidewalk seating perfect for people-watching, and wide selection of wines and cocktails.

Eataly Boston:

- Address: 800 Boylston St, Boston, MA 02199
- Phone: +1 617-807-7300
- Website: www.eataly.com
- Hours: Monday-Sunday 8:00 AM - 10:00 PM

A culinary paradise featuring a variety of Italian delicacies, including fresh pasta, gourmet pizza, gelato, and a vast selection of Italian wines. Eataly offers a vibrant ambience, food counters, and a market where you can purchase authentic Italian ingredients.

Top of the Hub:

- Address: 800 Boylston St, 52nd floor, Boston, MA 02199
- Phone: +1 617-536-1775
- Website: www.topofthehub.net
- Hours: Sunday-Thursday 11:30 AM - 1:00 AM, Friday-Saturday 11:30 AM - 2:00 AM

Located on the 52nd floor of the Prudential Tower, this upscale restaurant offers breathtaking panoramic views of the city. Enjoy a fine dining experience with a menu featuring seafood, steak, and New American cuisine.

Legal Sea Foods:

- Address: 800 Boylston St, Boston, MA 02199
- Phone: +1 617-266-6800
- Website: www.legalseafoods.com
- Hours: Monday-Sunday 11:30 AM - 9:00 PM

A Boston institution known for its fresh seafood and award-winning clam chowder. Legal Sea Foods serves a wide range of seafood dishes, including lobster, fish, and shellfish, in a lively and casual atmosphere.

The Courtyard Restaurant:

- Address: Boston Public Library, 700 Boylston St, Boston, MA 02116
- Phone: +1 617-859-2251
- Website: www.thecateredaffair.com
- Hours: Monday-Saturday 10:00 AM - 5:00 PM, Sunday 12:00 PM - 5:00 PM

Located within the Boston Public Library, The Courtyard Restaurant offers a charming setting with views of the library's picturesque courtyard. Enjoy a variety of light fare, sandwiches, salads, and desserts while immersing yourself in the library's ambience.

Atlantic Fish Co:

- Address: 761 Boylston St, Boston, MA 02116
- Phone: +1 617-267-4000
- Website: www.atlanticfish.com
- Hours: Monday-Sunday 11:30 AM - 10:00 PM

Indulge in fresh seafood at Atlantic Fish Co, known for its top-quality fish, oysters, and shellfish. With a warm and inviting ambience, this restaurant offers an extensive menu featuring classic New England seafood dishes and a wide selection of wines.

CHAPTER 3

EXPLORING BOSTON: BEACON HILL

Massachusetts State House

The Massachusetts State House is a historic landmark and the seat of the state government of Massachusetts. Located on Beacon Hill, the State House is known for its iconic golden dome and rich history. A visit to this architectural gem offers an opportunity to learn about Massachusetts' political heritage, admire stunning architecture, and enjoy panoramic views of the city.

Why Go:

The Massachusetts State House is a symbol of the state's democratic principles and serves as a living testament to its rich history. Exploring its halls and chambers allows visitors to delve into the state's political past and present. The grandeur of the building, its architectural details, and the significance of the decisions made within its walls make it an essential stop for history enthusiasts, architecture lovers, and anyone interested in understanding the state's governance.

When to Go:

The Massachusetts State House is open year-round for visitors. The best time to visit is on weekdays when the legislature is in session, offering a chance to observe the democratic process in action. However, even on weekends or during recess, visitors can explore the building's public areas, including the Hall of Flags and the Senate and House chambers. It's advisable to check the State House's website for specific visiting hours and any temporary closures due to events or maintenance.

Outdoor Activities:

Beacon Hill Walking Tour:

Take a stroll through Beacon Hill, the historic neighbourhood surrounding the State House. Explore its charming cobblestone streets, elegant brownstone houses, and picturesque Acorn Street, often considered one of the most photographed streets in America.

Boston Common:

Just a short walk from the State House, Boston Common is the oldest public park in the United States. Enjoy a leisurely walk, have a picnic, or relax on the park's green lawns. In winter, the Frog Pond in Boston Common transforms into an ice skating rink, offering seasonal fun for visitors of all ages.

Esplanade Park:

Located along the Charles River, the Esplanade Park offers scenic views, walking paths, and opportunities for biking, jogging, and picnicking.

Charles Street

Charles Street is a charming thoroughfare located in the heart of Boston's historic Beacon Hill neighbourhood. Lined with picturesque brick buildings, boutique shops, and inviting cafes, it offers a quintessential New England experience. Visitors can wander along its cobblestone sidewalks, discover unique treasures, indulge in delicious treats, and soak in the historic ambience of this iconic street.

Why Go:

Charles Street is a must-visit destination for those seeking a blend of history, shopping, and local charm. It's historic significance and well-preserved architecture make it an ideal spot for history enthusiasts and architecture lovers. The street's eclectic mix of boutiques, antique shops, and speciality stores offers a delightful shopping experience.

Additionally, its cosy cafes and restaurants provide the perfect setting to relax and soak up the vibrant atmosphere of Beacon Hill.

When to Go:

Charles Street is bustling year-round, but the best time to visit is during the spring and fall when the weather is mild and pleasant. The street comes alive with colourful flowers in bloom, and the surrounding foliage adds to its picturesque appeal. However, each season brings its charm, whether it's the festive decorations during the holiday season or the warm ambience of summer.

Outdoor Activities:
Public Garden:

Just a short walk from Charles Street, the Public Garden is a serene oasis with manicured lawns, vibrant flower beds, and a picturesque lagoon. Take a stroll, ride the iconic swan boats, or simply relax and enjoy the beauty of this urban sanctuary.

Louisburg Square:

Located near Charles Street, Louisburg Square is one of Boston's most exclusive addresses. Admire the elegant townhouses and picturesque surroundings as you wander through this tranquil square, which is often considered one of the city's hidden gems.

The Freedom Trail:

Charles Street is part of the iconic Freedom Trail, a 2.5-mile route that takes you through Boston's historic sites. Follow the red-brick path and explore significant landmarks, including the Massachusetts State House, Paul Revere's House, and the Old North Church.

Acorn Street

Tucked away in Boston's historic Beacon Hill neighbourhood, Acorn Street is a postcard-perfect cobblestone lane known for its picturesque charm. This narrow and enchanting street captures the essence of old-world Boston with its beautifully preserved rowhouses, gas lamps, and a captivating ambience. Acorn Street is a beloved destination for both locals and visitors seeking a glimpse into the city's rich history and architectural beauty.

Why Go:

Acorn Street is a must-visit for its timeless beauty and historical significance. Walking along this iconic street feels like stepping back in time, offering a unique opportunity to experience Boston's colonial past. The well-preserved cobblestones, red brick facades, and quaint atmosphere make it an ideal spot for history enthusiasts, photographers, and those seeking an enchanting escape from the bustling city.

When to Go:

Acorn Street is a year-round destination, each season offering its charm. Spring brings blooming flowers and a burst of colour to the street, while summer showcases the lush foliage and warm sunshine. Fall treats visitors to a picturesque display of autumn colours, and winter blankets the area with a quiet charm, especially after a fresh snowfall. Regardless of the season, Acorn Street is always a sight to behold.

Outdoor Activities:

Beacon Hill Garden Club Hidden Gardens:

Beacon Hill Garden Club organizes an annual Hidden Gardens tour, allowing visitors to discover the private gardens hidden within the neighbourhood. Explore these secret havens and admire the meticulously manicured landscapes during this special event.

Black Heritage Trail:

Embark on a self-guided walking tour along the Black Heritage Trail, which passes through Beacon Hill. This trail highlights significant sites and stories related to Boston's African American community, providing insights into the city's rich history and culture.

Boston Common, located in the heart of the city, is a historic public park that holds a significant place in Boston's history and culture. Established in 1634, it is the oldest public park in the United States and has played a vital role in the community for centuries. With its expansive green spaces, scenic views, iconic landmarks, and a wealth of recreational opportunities, Boston Common is a beloved destination for locals and visitors alike.

Why Go: A visit to Boston Common offers a multifaceted experience. It provides a serene retreat from the bustling city, where visitors can relax, unwind, and immerse themselves in nature. The park also serves as a gathering place for community events, festivals, and public gatherings throughout the year. Moreover, Boston

Common holds historical significance as a site for protests, speeches, and political demonstrations, making it a symbol of freedom and civic engagement.

When to Go: Boston Common is accessible year-round and offers a different ambience with each season. In spring, the park blooms with vibrant flowers and blossoming trees, creating a picturesque setting. Summer welcomes visitors with warm weather, providing an ideal backdrop for picnics, outdoor concerts, and recreational activities. Fall transforms the park into a mesmerizing palette of autumn colours, offering scenic beauty for leisurely walks. Winter blankets the Common with snow, creating a charming atmosphere for ice skating on the Frog Pond and enjoying seasonal events.

Outdoor Activities:

Swan Boat Rides:

Take a leisurely ride on the iconic Swan Boats in the Public Garden adjacent to Boston Common. These pedal-powered boats offer a unique way to enjoy the park's serene atmosphere while gliding across the tranquil waters.

The Soldiers and Sailors Monument:

Located within Boston Common, the Soldiers and Sailors Monument is a majestic memorial honouring the soldiers and sailors who fought in the Civil War. Climb to the top for panoramic views of the park and the city skyline.

Public Garden:

Adjacent to Boston Common, the Public Garden is a meticulously manicured botanical garden with enchanting pathways, beautiful flower beds, and a picturesque lagoon. Take a stroll, enjoy a picnic, or simply relax amidst the tranquil surroundings.

Fifteen Beacon:

- Address: 15 Beacon St, Boston, MA 02108
- Phone: +1 617-670-1500
- Website: www.xvbeacon.com

Located just a short walk from the State House, Fifteen Beacon is a luxury boutique hotel offering elegant accommodations. With its stylish rooms, attentive service, and proximity to Beacon Hill's attractions, it provides a refined and comfortable stay.

Beacon Hill Hotel and Bistro:

- Address: 25 Charles St, Boston, MA 02114
- Phone: +1 617-865-8020
- Website: www.beaconhillhotel.com

This charming boutique hotel captures the essence of Beacon Hill's historic neighbourhood. Its cosy rooms, welcoming atmosphere, and onsite bistro serving classic New England cuisine offer a delightful stay near the State House.

XV Beacon Hotel:

- Address: 15 Beacon St, Boston, MA 02108
- Phone: +1 617-670-1500
- Website: www.xvbeacon.com

Located just a short walk from Acorn Street, XV Beacon Hotel offers luxurious accommodations in a historic setting. With elegant rooms, exceptional service, and modern amenities, it provides a refined and comfortable stay in the heart of Beacon Hill.

The Liberty Hotel:

- Address: 215 Charles St, Boston, MA 02114
- Phone: +1 617-224-4000
- Website: www.libertyhotel.com

Housed in a beautifully restored historic building, The Liberty Hotel offers a unique blend of history and luxury. Situated near Charles Street, it provides easy access to the vibrant street and features upscale rooms, fine dining options, and a rooftop bar with breathtaking views.

The Godfrey Hotel Boston:

- Address: 505 Washington St, Boston, MA 02111
- Phone: +1 617-804-2000
- Website: www.godfreyhotelboston.com

Located near Boston Common, The Godfrey Hotel offers contemporary and stylish accommodations with modern amenities. Its central location makes it convenient for exploring the park and other nearby attractions. The hotel features comfortable rooms, a fitness centre, and an onsite restaurant for a comfortable and enjoyable stay.

The Ritz-Carlton, Boston:

- Address: 10 Avery St, Boston, MA 02111
- Phone: +1 617-574-7100
- Website: www.ritzcarlton.com

Nestled in the bustling downtown area, The Ritz-Carlton offers luxurious accommodations with impeccable service. The hotel boasts elegant rooms, a spa, fine dining options, and a convenient location within walking distance of Boston Common and other notable landmarks.

Kimpton Nine Zero Hotel:

- Address: 90 Tremont St, Boston, MA 02108
- Phone: +1 617-772-5800
- Website: www.ninezero.com

Just steps away from Boston Common, Kimpton Nine Zero Hotel combines contemporary design with exceptional service. The hotel offers stylish rooms, a fitness centre, and a trendy rooftop lounge with panoramic views of the city, providing a comfortable and memorable stay near the park.

Scampo:

- Address: 215 Charles St, Boston, MA 02114
- Phone: +1 617-536-2100
- Website: www.scampoboston.com
- Hours: Daily 7:00 AM - 10:00 PM

Located within The Liberty Hotel, Scampo is an upscale Italian restaurant helmed by award-winning chef Lydia Shire. Its creative menu features a blend of Italian and Mediterranean flavours, showcasing dishes like wood-fired pizzas, handmade pasta, and seafood specialities.

Grotto:

- Address: 37 Bowdoin St, Boston, MA 02114
- Phone: +1 617-227-3434
- Website: www.grottorestaurant.com
- Hours: Monday-Saturday 5:00 PM - 10:00 PM, Sunday 5:00 PM - 9:00 PM

Nestled in Beacon Hill, Grotto is a cosy Italian restaurant known for its intimate ambience and delectable cuisine. With a focus on seasonal ingredients, the menu offers classic Italian dishes with a modern twist, such as homemade pasta, wood-fired pizzas, and fresh seafood.

The Paramount:

- Address: 44 Charles St, Boston, MA 02114
- Phone: +1 617-720-1152
- Website: www.paramountboston.com
- Hours: Monday-Friday 7:00 AM - 9:00 PM, Saturday-Sunday 8:00 AM - 9:00 PM

A beloved neighbourhood spot, The Paramount serves up delicious comfort food in a casual setting. From hearty breakfast options to mouthwatering sandwiches, salads, and burgers, it offers a diverse menu that satisfies all appetites.

The Merchant:

- Address: 60 Franklin St, Boston, MA 02110
- Phone: +1 617-482-6060
- Website: www.themerchantboston.com
- Opening Hours: Monday-Friday 11:30 AM - 10:00 PM, Saturday-Sunday 4:00 PM - 10:00 PM

Located near Boston Common, The Merchant is a vibrant American brasserie that offers a diverse menu featuring fresh seafood, steaks, and creative cocktails. The restaurant's lively atmosphere, stylish decor, and delectable cuisine make it a popular dining spot for locals and visitors alike.

Tatte Bakery & Cafe:

- Address: 70 Charles St, Boston, MA 02114
- Phone: +1 617-723-5555
- Website: www.tattebakery.com
- Opening Hours: Monday-Sunday 8:00 AM - 6:00 PM

Tatte Bakery & Cafe is a beloved neighbourhood spot known for its delicious pastries, savoury sandwiches, and artisanal coffee. The cosy atmosphere, delectable menu, and inviting outdoor seating make it a perfect place to start your day or enjoy a leisurely break.

Figs:

- Address: 42 Charles St, Boston, MA 02114
- Phone: +1 617-742-3447
- Website: www.figsboston.com

- Opening Hours: Monday-Sunday 11:30 AM - 10:00 PM

Fig is a popular eatery specializing in wood-fired pizzas and creative Italian-inspired dishes. With its warm and inviting ambience, friendly service, and mouthwatering menu, it's a go-to spot for a casual and delicious dining experience on Charles Street.

Panificio Bistro & Bakery:
- Address: 144 Charles St, Boston, MA 02114
- Phone: +1 617-227-4340
- Website: www.panificioboston.com
- Opening Hours: Monday-Sunday 7:00 AM - 8:00 PM

Panificio offers a delightful combination of a bakery and bistro, serving up fresh pastries, sandwiches, salads, and more. Whether you're in the mood for a quick bite or a leisurely meal, this cosy eatery on Charles Street has something for everyone.

CHAPTER 4

EXPLORING BOSTON: NORTH END

Historic Italian District

The Historic Italian District, also known as the North End, is a vibrant neighbourhood in Boston that is rich in history, culture, and culinary delights. With its narrow cobblestone streets, charming brownstone buildings, and an abundance of Italian restaurants, bakeries, and cafes, the North End offers visitors a unique and immersive experience. It is a place where past and present converge, showcasing the influence of Italian immigrants on Boston's heritage and culinary scene.

Why Go:

A visit to the Historic Italian District allows you to step into a world of Italian culture and heritage right in the heart of

Boston. The neighbourhood is renowned for its authentic Italian cuisine, from mouthwatering pasta dishes and wood-fired pizzas to delectable pastries and gelato. Exploring the North End provides an opportunity to stroll along the historic streets, admire the architecture, and discover hidden gems such as charming boutiques, speciality shops, and cosy cafes. It's a place to indulge in delicious food, experience warm hospitality, and soak in the lively atmosphere of Boston's Italian heritage.

When to Go:

The Historic Italian District is bustling year-round, but certain times offer unique experiences. The summer months bring vibrant street festivals, such as the famous Saint Anthony's Feast in June and the Fisherman's Feast in August, where the neighbourhood comes alive with music, parades, and traditional processions. Fall brings cooler temperatures and the chance to witness the neighbourhood adorned with festive decorations during the Columbus Day celebrations. Winter offers a cosy ambience, with holiday lights adorning the streets and an array of seasonal treats to savour.

Outdoor Activities:

Paul Revere Mall:

Located in the heart of the North End, Paul Revere Mall, also known as the Prado, is a charming outdoor space adorned with statues and greenery. Take a leisurely walk through the mall, admire the sculptures, and enjoy the serene atmosphere.

Christopher Columbus Waterfront Park:

Situated along Boston Harbor, Christopher Columbus Waterfront Park offers breathtaking views, waterfront promenades, and open spaces for picnicking and relaxation.

Paul Revere House

The Paul Revere House is a historic landmark located in the North End neighbourhood of Boston. It holds great significance as the former home of American patriot Paul Revere, who played a crucial role in the American Revolutionary War. Today, the Paul Revere House stands as a testament to Boston's rich history and offers visitors a glimpse into the life and times of this iconic figure.

Why Go:
Visiting the Paul Revere House allows you to step back in time and gain insight into the life of Paul Revere and his contributions to American history. As the oldest surviving structure in downtown Boston, the house provides a tangible link to the city's revolutionary past. Exploring the house gives you a chance to see period furnishings, artefacts, and exhibits that showcase the events leading up to the American Revolution. It's a fascinating experience that immerses you in the sights and stories of Boston's revolutionary era.

When to Go:

The Paul Revere House is open to the public year-round, making it accessible for visitors at any time. However, to make the most of your visit, consider going during the quieter hours to fully appreciate the exhibits and take your time exploring. Weekdays, especially in the morning, are generally less crowded. Additionally, visiting in the spring or fall offers pleasant weather for exploring the surrounding neighbourhood and nearby attractions.

Outdoor Activities:

Paul Revere Mall:

Located adjacent to the Paul Revere House, Paul Revere Mall, also known as the Prado, is a charming outdoor space adorned with statues and greenery. Take a leisurely walk through the mall, admire the sculptures, and enjoy the serene atmosphere.

Boston Common:

Boston Common, located just a short distance from the Paul Revere House, is the oldest public park in the United States.

Freedom Trail: The Paul Revere House is part of the renowned Freedom Trail, a 2.5-mile-long trail that winds through Boston's historic sites.

Mike's Pastry

Mike's Pastry is a renowned bakery located in the North End neighbourhood of Boston. With a history dating back to 1946, it has become an iconic destination for locals and visitors alike. Known for its delectable pastries and traditional Italian treats, Mike's Pastry offers a delightful culinary experience in the heart of Boston.

Why Go:

A visit to Mike's Pastry is a must for food enthusiasts and dessert lovers. The bakery has earned a reputation for its wide variety of pastries, including cannoli, biscotti, cakes, and more. Whether you have a sweet tooth or simply appreciate artisanal baked goods, Mike's Pastry offers a delicious taste of authentic Italian treats in a vibrant and bustling atmosphere.

When to Go:

Mike's Pastry is open daily, making it convenient to satisfy your cravings at any time. However, keep in mind that it can get crowded, especially during peak hours and weekends. To avoid long queues, consider visiting during weekdays or earlier in the morning. It's a perfect spot for breakfast, an afternoon treat, or a delightful dessert after dinner.

Top Pastries at Mike's Pastry:

- **Cannoli:** The cannoli at Mike's Pastry are legendary. These traditional Italian pastries consist of crispy, fried shells filled with sweet and creamy ricotta cheese. They come in various flavours, such as classic vanilla, chocolate-dipped, pistachio, and more. Each bite is a delightful combination of textures and flavours that will leave you craving for more.

- **Lobster Tail:** The lobster tail is a signature pastry at Mike's Pastry. Resembling the shape of a lobster's tail, this flaky pastry is filled with light and airy whipped cream, creating a delightful contrast of textures. It's a delicious treat that showcases the bakery's craftsmanship and culinary expertise.

- **Biscotti:** For a crunchy and flavorful treat, try the biscotti at Mike's Pastry. These twice-baked cookies are available in various flavours, including almond, chocolate, pistachio, and more. Enjoy them with a cup of coffee or indulge in their own right. The biscotti's crispness and rich flavours make them a perfect accompaniment to any beverage.

Mike's Pastry Contact Details:

- Address: 300 Hanover St, Boston, MA 02113
- Phone: +1 617-742-3050
- Website: www.mikespastry.com

Visiting Mike's Pastry allows you to experience the vibrant culinary scene in Boston's North End. Whether you're enjoying their famous cannoli, savouring a lobster tail, or exploring the array of biscotti flavours, you'll be treated to an indulgent and memorable culinary adventure.

Hanover Street

Hanover Street is a vibrant and historic thoroughfare located in the North End neighbourhood of Boston. It is known as the "Main Street" of the city's Italian district and offers a rich cultural experience, a charming atmosphere, and a wide array of dining options. From traditional Italian eateries to trendy cafes and shops, Hanover Street is a must-visit destination for food enthusiasts and those seeking an authentic taste of Boston's Italian heritage.

Why Go:

Hanover Street captures the essence of Boston's Italian culture, with its bustling energy, lively street life, and an abundance of delicious food. Whether you're strolling along the sidewalk, admiring the historic buildings, or indulging in Italian pastries and cuisine, Hanover Street offers a unique and immersive experience that showcases the vibrant spirit of the North End.

When to Go:

Hanover Street is bustling throughout the year, but it is particularly vibrant during weekends and evenings when locals and tourists gather to enjoy the lively atmosphere. If you prefer a quieter experience, consider visiting during weekdays or earlier in the day. Regardless of the time you choose, Hanover Street guarantees a delightful culinary adventure and a glimpse into the rich Italian heritage of Boston.

Battery Wharf Hotel:
- Address: 3 Battery Wharf, Boston, MA 02109
- Phone: +1 617-994-9000
- Website:www.batterywharfhotelboston.com

Located near the Historic Italian District, Battery Wharf Hotel offers luxurious waterfront accommodations with stunning views of the harbour. The hotel features elegant rooms, a spa, a fitness centre, and an onsite restaurant, providing a tranquil and upscale retreat after a day of exploring the neighbourhood.

Boston Yacht Haven:
- Address: 87 Commercial Wharf, Boston, MA 02110
- Phone: +1 617-367-5050
- Website: www.yachthavenboston.com

For a unique and memorable experience, consider staying at Boston Yacht Haven, a boutique hotel located along the waterfront near the North End. The hotel offers stylish rooms with nautical-themed decor and marina views. It provides easy access to the neighbourhood's attractions and offers a marina for guests arriving by boat.

The Boxer Boston:
- Address: 107 Merrimac St, Boston, MA 02114
- Phone: +1 617-624-0202
- Website: www.theboxerboston.com

Situated in the nearby Bulfinch Triangle, The Boxer Boston is a boutique hotel that offers a blend of modern comfort and historic charm. The hotel features well-appointed rooms, a fitness centre, and a convenient location within walking distance of the North End, making it an ideal base for exploring the neighbourhood.

Omni Parker House:
- Address: 60 School St, Boston, MA 02108
- Phone: +1 617-227-8600
- Website:www.omnihotels.com/hotels/boston-parker-house

The Omni Parker House is a historic hotel located in the heart of downtown Boston. It offers elegant accommodations, classic charm, and a prime location near the Paul Revere House and other major attractions. With its rich history and impeccable service, it provides a memorable stay for history buffs.

Neptune Oyster:

- Address: 63 Salem St, Boston, MA 02113
- Phone: +1 617-742-3474
- Opening Hours: Monday-Saturday 11:30 AM - 10:00 PM, Sunday 12:00 PM - 9:00 PM

Known for its outstanding seafood, Neptune Oyster is a popular restaurant in the North End. This cosy eatery offers a variety of fresh oysters, lobster rolls, and other seafood delicacies, all served with a touch of New England flair. Be prepared for a wait, as it's a small and highly sought-after spot.

Mamma Maria:

- Address: 3 North Square, Boston, MA 02113
- Phone: +1 617-523-0077
- Opening Hours: Monday-Saturday 5:00 PM - 10:00 PM, Sunday 4:30 PM - 9:30 PM

Mamma Maria is a charming Italian restaurant that offers a cosy and romantic ambience. It serves authentic Italian dishes made with seasonal ingredients, including homemade pasta, succulent meats, and delectable desserts. The attentive service and warm atmosphere make it a favourite among locals and visitors alike.

Mike's Pastry:

- Address: 300 Hanover St, Boston, MA 02113
- Phone: +1 617-742-3050
- Opening Hours: Sunday-Thursday 8:00 AM - 10:00 PM, Friday-Saturday 8:00 AM - 11:00 PM

No visit to the Historic Italian District is complete without indulging in the delightful pastries and desserts at Mike's Pastry. This iconic bakery offers a wide selection of cannoli, biscotti, cakes, and other sweet treats that will satisfy any sweet tooth. Be prepared for a line, as it's a popular spot, but the delicious pastries are worth the wait.

Regina Pizzeria:

- Address: 11 1/2 Thacher St, Boston, MA 02113
- Phone: +1 617-227-0765
- Opening Hours: Sunday-Thursday 11:00 AM - 10:00 PM, Friday-Saturday 11:00 AM - 11:00 PM

Located just a short walk from the Paul Revere House, Regina Pizzeria is a must-visit for pizza lovers. It has been serving delicious, authentic Neapolitan-style pizzas since 1926. With its cosy atmosphere and mouthwatering toppings, it's the perfect spot for a satisfying meal after exploring the historic site.

Modern Pastry Shop:
- Address: 257 Hanover St, Boston, MA 02113
- Phone: +1 617-523-3783
- Opening Hours: Sunday-Thursday 8:00 AM - 10:00 PM, Friday-Saturday 8:00 AM - 11:00 PM

No visit to the North End is complete without indulging in the delightful pastries at Modern Pastry Shop. This beloved bakery has been serving an array of Italian pastries, cakes, and cookies since 1930. Whether you crave cannoli, tiramisu, or biscotti, this bakery is a true delight for your taste buds.

Modern Pastry:

- Address: 257 Hanover St, Boston, MA 02113
- Phone: +1 617-523-3783
- Website: www.modernpastry.com

Located right on Hanover Street, Modern Pastry is a beloved bakery offering a wide variety of Italian pastries, cakes, and cookies. Their cannoli are particularly famous, with crispy shells and rich, creamy fillings. From traditional flavours to inventive variations like Nutella and Limoncello, Modern Pastry ensures a delightful and indulgent dessert experience.

CHAPTER 5

EXPLORING BOSTON: FENWAY-
KENMORE

Fenway Park

Fenway Park is an iconic baseball stadium located in the Fenway-Kenmore neighbourhood of Boston. It is not only the oldest ballpark in Major League Baseball but also a beloved historic landmark that holds a special place in the hearts of Bostonians and baseball enthusiasts worldwide. With its rich history, unique architecture, and passionate fan base, Fenway Park offers a one-of-a-kind experience for sports fans and visitors alike.

Why Go: A visit to Fenway Park is a must for sports enthusiasts, baseball fans, and anyone interested in experiencing the vibrant sports culture of Boston. The stadium's rich history, legendary moments, and passionate atmosphere create an electric energy that is truly captivating. Whether you're catching a game, taking a guided tour, or simply exploring the surrounding area, Fenway Park provides an immersive and memorable experience that showcases the city's deep-rooted love for its baseball team, the Boston Red Sox.

When to Go: The baseball season typically runs from April to September, with occasional games in October for postseason play. Attending a game during the regular season allows you to witness the excitement and cheer alongside dedicated Red Sox fans. However, even if you're visiting outside of the baseball season, Fenway Park offers guided tours that provide behind-the-scenes access, historical insights, and a chance to explore the stadium's iconic features.

Best Outdoor Activities near Fenway Park:
Yawkey Way: Yawkey Way, renamed Jersey Street, is a pedestrian-friendly area adjacent to Fenway Park. It offers

a festive atmosphere on game days, with street vendors, live music, and an opportunity to soak in the pre-game excitement. Strolling along Yawkey Way is a great way to immerse yourself in the baseball culture and engage with fellow fans.

The Fenway Victory Gardens: Located near Fenway Park, the Fenway Victory Gardens is a beautiful and historic community garden. Visitors can take a stroll through the gardens, admire the vibrant flowers and greenery, and learn about its significance as a symbol of community resilience during World War II. It's a peaceful oasis in the heart of the city.

Emerald Necklace: The Emerald Necklace is a series of interconnected parks and green spaces that includes the famous Boston Common and the adjacent Public Garden. Visitors can enjoy a leisurely walk or bike ride along the park's trails, or take a swan boat ride in the Public Garden, which relax amidst the natural beauty that surrounds Fenway Park.

Isabella Stewart Gardner Museum

The Isabella Stewart Gardner Museum is a hidden gem nestled in the Fenway-Kenmore neighbourhood of Boston. This enchanting museum showcases an extraordinary collection of art and offers visitors a unique and immersive experience. From stunning architecture to carefully curated works of art, the Gardner Museum is a must-visit destination for art enthusiasts and culture lovers alike.

Why Go:

The Isabella Stewart Gardner Museum is renowned for its remarkable collection, which spans various periods and styles, including European, Asian, and American art. It is home to masterpieces by renowned artists such as Rembrandt, Vermeer, and Botticelli. Beyond the art, the museum's architecture and lush courtyard garden create an enchanting atmosphere that transports visitors to another time and place. A visit to the Gardner Museum offers an opportunity to appreciate art, immerse oneself in history, and experience the vision of its founder, Isabella Stewart Gardner.

When to Go:

The museum is open year-round, and each season brings its unique charm. Spring and summer allow for a leisurely exploration of the outdoor spaces, including the beautiful courtyard garden. Fall showcases the vibrant colours of the surrounding foliage, providing a picturesque backdrop to the museum. Winter offers a cosy and intimate atmosphere, perfect for appreciating art and architecture.

Outdoor Activities near the Isabella Stewart Gardner Museum:

Explore the Fens:

Adjacent to the museum, the Fens is a picturesque parkland featuring meandering paths, serene ponds, and beautiful landscaping. Take a stroll or bike ride through this urban oasis, appreciating the greenery and tranquillity it offers. Spring and fall are particularly lovely seasons to explore the Fens.

Visit the Back Bay Fens:

Just a short walk from the museum, the Back Bay Fens is a part of the larger Emerald Necklace Park system. It offers vast open spaces, athletic fields, and a picturesque rose garden. Enjoy a picnic, play sports, or simply relax in this expansive green space during the warmer months.

Discover the Riverway: The Riverway is another section of the Emerald Necklace that runs parallel to the Muddy River. Riverway is ideal for walking, jogging, or cycling. Immerse yourself in the natural beauty of this urban park, and enjoy the tranquillity it provides away from the bustling city streets.

Symphony Hall is a world-renowned concert venue located in the Fenway-Kenmore neighbourhood of Boston. As the home of the Boston Symphony Orchestra, it has a rich history and is celebrated for its exceptional acoustics. Symphony Hall offers visitors the opportunity to experience unforgettable live performances by renowned musicians and orchestras from around the world.

Why Go: Symphony Hall is a must-visit destination for music lovers and cultural enthusiasts. It is recognized as one of the finest concert halls in the world, known for its exceptional sound quality and architectural beauty. Attending a concert at Symphony Hall allows you to witness the power and artistry of live classical music performances in a setting designed to enhance the acoustics and create a truly immersive experience.

When to Go: Symphony Hall hosts concerts throughout the year, offering a diverse range of performances. From symphony orchestras and chamber music ensembles to solo recitals and guest performances, there is always something captivating happening at Symphony Hall. Check the concert schedule in advance to plan your visit around the performances that interest you the most.

Outdoor Activities near Symphony Hall:
Explore the Back Bay Fens: Adjacent to Symphony Hall, the Back Bay Fens is part of the renowned Emerald Necklace Park system.

Visit Fenway Park:
Just a short walk from Symphony Hall, Fenway Park is a historic baseball stadium and home to the Boston Red Sox. Catch a game during baseball season or take a guided tour to learn about the stadium's fascinating history and soak in the atmosphere of this iconic sports venue.

Shop and Dine on Newbury Street:
Explore Newbury Street, a vibrant shopping destination lined with boutique stores, art galleries, cafes, and restaurants. Indulge in some retail therapy, savour delicious meals, and experience the lively atmosphere of

this bustling street, all within walking distance of Symphony Hall.

Best Places to Stay @Fenway-Kenmore

02215 Bay/Fenway:

- Address: 125 Brookline Ave, Boston, MA 02215
- Phone: +1 617-236-8787
- Website: www.marriott.com/bosbb

This all-suite hotel is located within walking distance of Fenway Park, making it an ideal choice for baseball fans. With spacious suites, fully equipped kitchens, and complimentary breakfast, Residence Inn offers a comfortable and convenient stay for both short and extended visits.

Verb Hotel:

- Address: 1271 Boylston St, Boston, MA 02215
- Phone: +1 617-566-4500
- Website: www.theverbhotel.com

The Verb Hotel is a unique boutique hotel with a retro rock 'n' roll theme, paying homage to the music history of Boston. Situated near Fenway Park, it offers stylish rooms, a vibrant atmosphere, and an outdoor pool, creating a memorable and lively stay experience for guests.

Best Places to Stay near the Isabella Stewart Gardner Museum:

The Eliot Hotel:

- Address: 370 Commonwealth Ave, Boston, MA 02215
- Phone: +1 617-267-1607
- Website: www.eliothotel.com

The Eliot Hotel is a luxurious boutique hotel located in the Back Bay neighbourhood, just a short distance from the museum. With elegant rooms, attentive service, and a sophisticated atmosphere, it provides a comfortable and memorable stay experience.

Hotel Commonwealth:

- Address: 500 Commonwealth Ave, Boston, MA 02215
- Phone: +1 617-933-5000
- Website: www.hotelcommonwealth.com

Situated in the heart of Kenmore Square, Hotel Commonwealth offers modern accommodations and easy access to the Gardner Museum. With its stylish rooms, convenient amenities, and proximity to nearby attractions, it is an ideal choice for travellers seeking comfort and convenience.

The Colonnade Hotel:

- Address: 120 Huntington Ave, Boston, MA 02116
- Phone: +1 617-424-7000
- Website: www.colonnadehotel.com

Located in the Back Bay neighbourhood, The Colonnade Hotel offers stylish accommodations and modern amenities. Its central location provides easy access to Symphony Hall and other nearby attractions. Enjoy comfortable rooms, a rooftop pool, and exceptional service during your stay.

Thornton's Restaurant:

- Address: 401 Massachusetts Ave, Boston, MA 02115
- Opening Hours: Tuesday-Saturday: 5:00 PM - 10:00 PM
- Website: www.thorntonsfenway.com

Adjacent to Symphony Hall, Thornton's Restaurant offers a refined dining experience with a focus on seasonal and locally sourced ingredients. The menu features a range of innovative dishes and classic favourites, complemented by an extensive wine selection.

Sweet Cheeks Q:

- Address: 1381 Boylston St, Boston, MA 02215
- Opening Hours: Monday-Sunday: 11:30 AM - 10:00 PM
- Website: www.sweetcheeksq.com

For a casual and delicious dining option near Symphony Hall, head to Sweet Cheeks Q. This barbecue joint serves up mouthwatering Southern-style dishes, including smoked meats, tasty sides, and delectable desserts. Enjoy a laid-back atmosphere and indulge in hearty comfort food.

Basho Japanese Brasserie:
- Address: 1338 Boylston St, Boston, MA 02215
- Opening Hours: Monday-Sunday: 11:30 AM - 10:00 PM
- Website: www.bashosushi.com

Located a short distance from Symphony Hall, Basho Japanese Brasserie offers a diverse menu of authentic Japanese cuisine. From sushi and sashimi to hot dishes and speciality cocktails, this restaurant delights guests with its traditional flavours and contemporary presentations.

Café G:
- Address: 25 Evans Way, Boston, MA 02115
- Opening Hours: Tuesday-Sunday: 11:00 AM - 4:30 PM
- Website: www.gardnermuseum.org/visit/cafe-g

Located within the museum itself, Café G offers a delightful dining experience amidst the beautiful surroundings. It serves a variety of light bites, sandwiches, salads, and beverages, making it a perfect spot for a quick refreshment during your museum visit.

Eastern Standard:
- Address: 528 Commonwealth Ave, Boston, MA 02215
- Opening Hours: Daily: 7:00 AM - 2:00 AM
- Website: www.easternstandardboston.com

Just a short walk from the museum, Eastern Standard is a popular restaurant known for its classic American cuisine and lively atmosphere. It offers a diverse menu featuring dishes made from locally sourced ingredients, as well as an extensive drink selection.

Island Creek Oyster Bar:
- Address: 500 Commonwealth Ave, Boston, MA 02215
- Opening Hours: Monday-Sunday: 11:30 AM - 10:00 PM
- Website: www.islandcreekoysterbar.com

Located in the vibrant Kenmore Square, Island Creek Oyster Bar specializes in seafood and offers a range of delectable dishes, including fresh oysters, seafood platters, and innovative seafood preparations. The restaurant's stylish ambience and exceptional service create a memorable dining experience.

CHAPTER 6

MUST-SEE ATTRACTIONS

Freedom Trail

The Freedom Trail is a historic 2.5-mile (4-kilometre) trail that winds through downtown Boston, connecting 16 significant historical sites. It is a must-visit attraction for history enthusiasts and anyone interested in exploring the rich heritage of the city. The trail takes you on a journey through the American Revolution, showcasing iconic landmarks, museums, churches, and burial grounds that played pivotal roles in shaping the nation's history.

Outdoor Activities along the Freedom Trail:
Walking the Trail:
The Freedom Trail is best experienced on foot. Embark on a self-guided or guided tour and follow the red-brick or painted line that marks the trail's path. As you walk, immerse yourself in the stories of the American Revolution and learn about the events that unfolded in each location.

Enjoy the scenic streets of Boston while retracing the footsteps of historical figures.

Boston Common:

Start your Freedom Trail journey at Boston Common, the oldest public park in the United States. This picturesque green space offers a tranquil escape from the bustling city. Take a leisurely stroll, have a picnic, or relax on the lawns. The park also hosts seasonal events and concerts, providing additional entertainment for visitors.

Bunker Hill Monument and Charlestown Navy Yard:

Visit the Bunker Hill Monument and Charlestown Navy Yard, located across the Charles River from downtown Boston. Climb the 294 steps to the top of the Bunker Hill Monument for panoramic views of the city skyline. Explore the Charlestown Navy Yard, which houses the USS Constitution Museum and the historic USS Constitution ("Old Ironsides") itself. Learn about the naval history of the United States and see the world's oldest commissioned warship still afloat.

USS Constitution Museum:

Located in the Charlestown Navy Yard, the USS Constitution Museum provides insight into the history of the USS Constitution and its role in defending the nation. Discover interactive exhibits, artefacts, and engaging displays that showcase the stories of sailors, shipbuilding, and the Constitution's remarkable victories.

Paul Revere's House and Old North Church:

Step into the footsteps of American patriot Paul Revere by visiting his former home, now the Paul Revere's House museum. Experience life in the 18th century and learn about Revere's famous midnight ride. Just a short walk away is the Old North Church, where lanterns were hung to signal the British army's movements. Explore the church's history and admire its iconic steeple.

Granary Burying Ground:

Pay your respects to notable figures from American history at the Granary Burying Ground. This historic cemetery is the final resting place of prominent individuals such as Paul Revere, John Hancock, Samuel Adams, and many more. Walk among the gravestones and reflect on the significance of those who contributed to the birth of a nation.

Faneuil Hall and Quincy Market:

Conclude your Freedom Trail adventure by visiting Faneuil Hall and Quincy Market. Faneuil Hall, often referred to as the "Cradle of Liberty," has served as a marketplace and a site for public meetings and speeches since the 18th century. Explore the vibrant Quincy Market, filled with shops, restaurants, and food stalls offering a variety of culinary delights.

Exploring the Freedom Trail is a journey through the pages of American history.

Boston Harbor, located on the eastern coast of Massachusetts, is a vibrant and historically significant area that offers a multitude of attractions and outdoor activities. As a top attraction in Boston, the harbour is a haven for maritime enthusiasts, nature lovers, and those seeking unique experiences along the waterfront. With its rich history, scenic beauty, and diverse offerings, Boston Harbor is a must-visit destination for locals and tourists alike.

Boston Harbor Islands:

The Boston Harbor Islands, a collection of 34 islands and peninsulas, provide a tranquil escape from the bustling city. These islands offer opportunities for hiking, picnicking, swimming, and exploring historic sites. Visitors can take a ferry from Long Wharf or Hingham to reach popular islands such as Spectacle Island, Georges Island, and Deer Island. Each island has its own unique charm and recreational activities, making them perfect for a day trip or a weekend getaway.

Harborwalk:

The Harborwalk is a picturesque waterfront promenade that stretches for miles along Boston Harbor. This scenic pathway invites visitors to take leisurely strolls, jog, bike, or simply enjoy the breathtaking views. Along the way, you'll encounter public art installations, parks, gardens, and a variety of dining options. The Harborwalk provides an excellent opportunity to immerse yourself in the beauty of the harbour while discovering the city's vibrant waterfront neighbourhoods.

New England Aquarium:

Situated on Central Wharf, the New England Aquarium is a premier marine attraction that delights visitors of all ages. Home to a wide array of aquatic species, including penguins, sea turtles, sharks, and colourful fish, the aquarium offers an immersive experience. Explore captivating exhibits, watch engaging presentations, and even have the chance to touch stingrays in the popular "Ray Touch Tank." The New England Aquarium is a must-visit destination for those seeking to learn about marine life and conservation efforts.

Whale-Watching Tours:

Embarking on a whale-watching tour from Boston Harbor is an unforgettable experience. These excursions take you out into the Atlantic Ocean, where you can witness magnificent marine creatures, such as humpback whales, finback whales, and dolphins, in their natural habitat. Knowledgeable guides provide insights into these magnificent creatures and their migratory patterns. Whale-watching tours typically operate from April to October, offering the best chance to spot these majestic animals.

Museum of Fine Arts

The Museum of Fine Arts (MFA) in Boston is a world-renowned cultural institution that showcases an extraordinary collection of art spanning thousands of years. As one of the top attractions in the city, the MFA offers visitors a captivating journey through diverse artistic styles, periods, and cultures. With its extensive permanent collections, special exhibitions, and engaging tours, the museum promises an enriching and inspiring experience for art enthusiasts and curious travellers alike.

Permanent Collections: The MFA boasts an impressive collection of over 450,000 artworks, representing various artistic disciplines and cultures from around the globe. From ancient Egyptian artefacts and classical Greek sculptures to European paintings and contemporary art, the museum's permanent collections offer a comprehensive survey of artistic expression throughout history. Visitors can admire renowned works by masters such as Monet, Rembrandt, Van Gogh, and Picasso, as well as explore lesser-known gems that celebrate the diversity of human creativity.

Special Exhibitions: In addition to its permanent collections, the MFA hosts a dynamic lineup of special exhibitions that showcase a range of artistic movements, themes, and mediums. These temporary exhibitions provide unique insights into specific periods, artists, or art forms, allowing visitors to delve deeper into specific areas of interest. With a rotating calendar of exhibitions, there's always something new and exciting to discover at the MFA, ensuring a fresh and engaging experience with each visit.

Art of the Americas Wing Tours: The Art of the Americas Wing at the MFA is a treasure trove of exceptional artworks from North, Central, and South America. To enhance the visitor experience, the museum offers guided tours of this expansive wing, providing valuable insights into the diverse cultures and artistic traditions of the Americas. Knowledgeable guides lead visitors through the galleries, highlighting key artworks and sharing captivating stories and interpretations. These tours offer a deeper understanding of the rich artistic heritage of the Americas, fostering a greater appreciation for the cultural tapestry of the region.

Outdoor Activities: While the main focus of the MFA is its exceptional indoor galleries, there are also outdoor activities that complement the museum experience. The museum's stunning courtyard, known as the Shapiro Family Courtyard, offers a serene and inviting space to relax and reflect amidst beautiful architectural surroundings. Visitors can enjoy a moment of tranquillity while appreciating the harmonious fusion of art and nature.

Visiting the Museum of Fine Arts allows you to immerse yourself in the captivating world of art, spanning centuries and continents. Explore the museum's permanent collections to encounter masterpieces from renowned artists, and be sure to check out the special exhibitions for a glimpse into specific artistic narratives.

Harvard University, nestled in the historic city of Cambridge just across the Charles River from Boston, is an iconic institution renowned for its academic excellence and rich history. As one of the top attractions in the Boston area, Harvard University offers visitors a chance to explore its picturesque campus, delve into world-class museums, immerse themselves in the vibrant atmosphere of Harvard Square, and even embark on a unique and entertaining "Hahvahd" Tour.

Harvard Yard:

At the heart of Harvard University lies Harvard Yard, a captivating green space surrounded by historic buildings and bustling with intellectual energy. This iconic symbol of the university invites visitors to stroll through its pathways, taking in the collegiate atmosphere and admiring the beautiful architecture. With its lush lawns, shaded trees, and iconic landmarks like the John Harvard Statue and Memorial Church, Harvard Yard is a must-see destination that captures the essence of this prestigious institution.

Harvard Museums:

Harvard University boasts a collection of world-class museums that cater to a wide range of interests. The Harvard Art Museums house an impressive collection of artworks from different cultures and periods, including renowned masterpieces by artists such as Rembrandt, Monet, and Van Gogh. The Harvard Museum of Natural History offers fascinating exhibits that explore the wonders of the natural world, including dinosaur fossils, gemstones, and the renowned Glass Flowers. These museums provide an enriching and educational experience, allowing visitors to engage with diverse subjects through the lens of art, history, and science.

Harvard Square:

Adjacent to the university campus, Harvard Square is a vibrant and lively neighbourhood filled with an array of shops, restaurants, cafes, and bookstores. This bustling cultural hub exudes an eclectic and bohemian atmosphere, attracting students, locals, and visitors alike. Stroll through the square's bustling streets, browse independent boutiques, savour diverse cuisine, or simply find a cosy spot to people-watch and soak up the lively ambience. Harvard Square is not only a place to explore, but also a prime spot to experience the vibrant energy and intellectual curiosity that defines Harvard University.

The Hahvahd Tour:

For a unique and entertaining experience, embark on The Hahvahd Tour, a guided exploration of Harvard University led by enthusiastic student guides. This entertaining tour offers an insider's perspective on campus life, showcasing iconic landmarks, historical anecdotes, and a playful take on the distinct Boston accent. Learn about Harvard's fascinating history, traditions, and notable alumni while immersing yourself in the vibrant atmosphere of one of the world's most prestigious educational institutions. The Hahvahd Tour promises an enjoyable and memorable way to discover the secrets and stories of Harvard University.

125

Visiting Harvard University provides an opportunity to step into the world of academia and explore the storied halls of one of the world's most prestigious universities. Take a stroll through Harvard Yard, soak up the intellectual atmosphere, and capture photos of iconic landmarks. Immerse yourself in art, history, and science at the Harvard Museums, expanding your knowledge and appreciation of the world around us. Experience the vibrant energy of Harvard Square, where history, culture, and youthful enthusiasm converge. And don't miss the chance to join The Hahvahd Tour for a lighthearted and informative journey through the university's captivating history.

CHAPTER 7

BOSTON FOR FOOD LOVERS

Seafood Delights

When it comes to seafood, Boston is a culinary paradise. With its proximity to the Atlantic Ocean, the city offers an abundance of fresh and delicious seafood options. Whether you're craving succulent lobster, crispy fried clams, or mouthwatering oysters, Boston's seafood scene has something to satisfy every palate. Here are some top seafood restaurants in Boston that are worth a visit:

Union Oyster House:

- Website: www.unionoysterhouse.com
- Contact: +1-617-227-2750
- Address: 41 Union Street, Boston, MA 02108
- Hours: Sun-Thur 11:00 am - 9:00 pm

  Fri & Sat 11:00 am - 10:00 pm

Established in 1826, the Union Oyster House is not only a historic landmark but also one of Boston's oldest and most beloved seafood establishments. This iconic restaurant offers a charming and nostalgic atmosphere, with cosy wooden booths and antique decor. Indulge in their famous clam chowder, freshly shucked oysters, or classic New England lobster dishes for an authentic taste of Boston's seafood heritage.

Legal Sea Foods:

- Website: www.legalseafoods.com
- Contact: +1-617-742-5300
- Address: Multiple locations in Boston
- Hours: Mon-Sat 10am - 10pm

With several locations throughout the city, Legal Sea Foods has become a Boston institution known for its commitment to quality seafood. This upscale seafood restaurant offers a diverse menu featuring everything from buttery baked scrod to tender grilled swordfish. Don't miss their signature dish, the New England clam chowder, which has received numerous accolades and is a true taste of Boston's seafood tradition.

Neptune Oyster:
- Website: www.neptuneoyster.com
- Contact: +1-617-742-3474
- Address: 63 Salem Street, Boston, MA 02113
- Hours: Mon- Sat 9am -9:30pm

For seafood lovers seeking an intimate and cosy dining experience, Neptune Oyster is a must-visit. Located in Boston's historic North End, this small seafood bar is known for its exceptional selection of oysters, lobster rolls, and other fresh seafood delicacies. Be prepared to wait for a table, as this hidden gem is popular among locals and visitors alike.

Atlantic Fish Company:

- Website: www.atlanticfishco.com
- Contact: +1-617-267-4000
- Address: 761 Boylston Street, Boston, MA 02116
- Hours: 10am - 11pm

Nestled in Boston's bustling Back Bay neighbourhood, Atlantic Fish Company offers a refined dining experience with a focus on classic seafood dishes. From their tender and flavorful grilled fish to their indulgent seafood paella, each dish is expertly prepared using the freshest ingredients. The elegant yet relaxed ambience makes it a great choice for a special seafood dining experience.

Ethnic Cuisine

Boston is a vibrant city that offers a diverse range of ethnic cuisines to tantalize your taste buds. From the charming Italian restaurants in the North End to the flavorful Asian flavours in Chinatown, and the cosy Irish pubs to the exotic Greek and Middle Eastern eateries, Boston's culinary scene has something for everyone. Here are some top restaurants in Boston where visitors can savour delicious ethnic cuisine:

Italian Restaurants in the North End:

Giacomo's Ristorante

- Website: www.giacomosblog-boston.blogspot.com
- Contact: +1-617-523-9026
- Address: 355 Hanover Street, Boston, MA 02113
- Hours: Monday-Saturday: 4:00 PM - 9:00 PM
- Sunday: 12:00 PM - 9:00 PM

Giacomo's Ristorante is a hidden gem in the heart of the North End, Boston's Little Italy. Known for its mouthwatering Italian dishes, this cosy restaurant serves up hearty portions of pasta, seafood, and classic Italian specialities. Be prepared for a wait, as it is a popular spot among locals and visitors alike.

Mamma Maria

- Website: www.mammamaria.com
- Contact: +1-617-523-0077
- Address: 3 North Square, Boston, MA 02113
- Hours: Monday-Sunday: 5:30 PM - 9:30 PM
- Price Range: $$$

Mamma Maria offers an elegant dining experience with its refined Italian cuisine and warm hospitality. Their menu features traditional Italian dishes made with seasonal and locally sourced ingredients. From homemade pasta to flavorful seafood preparations, Mamma Maria captures the essence of Italian culinary traditions.

Chinatown's Asian Flavors:

Gourmet Dumpling House

- Website: N/A
- Contact: +1-617-338-6223
- Address: 52 Beach Street, Boston, MA 02111
- Hours: Monday-Sunday: 10:00 AM - 10:00 PM

Gourmet Dumpling House is a beloved spot in Boston's Chinatown known for its authentic Chinese cuisine. From their delectable soup dumplings to their flavorful stir-fried dishes, every bite is bursting with authentic flavours. It's a popular choice for dim sum and a casual dining experience.

Irish Pubs and Eateries:

a) The Black Rose

- Website: www.blackroseboston.com
- Contact: +1-617-742-2286
- Address: 160 State Street, Boston, MA 02109
- Hours: Monday-Sunday: 11:00 AM - 2:00 AM

The Black Rose is a lively Irish pub located near Faneuil Hall Marketplace. This charming establishment offers a warm and welcoming atmosphere along with a menu featuring classic Irish dishes like fish and chips, shepherd's pie, and corned beef and cabbage. Enjoy live Irish music and a pint of Guinness for a truly authentic experience.

Greek and Middle Eastern Cuisine:

a) Oleana

- Website: www.oleanarestaurant.com

- Contact: +1-617-661-0505
- Address: 134 Hampshire Street, Cambridge, MA 02139
- Hours: Tuesday-Saturday: 5:30 PM - 9:30 PM

Located in Cambridge, just across the Charles River from Boston, Oleana is a Mediterranean-inspired restaurant offering a blend of Greek, Turkish, and Middle Eastern flavours. With its creative and vibrant dishes, Oleana takes diners on a culinary journey, highlighting the rich and diverse flavours of the Mediterranean region.

Local Specialties

When it comes to Boston's local specialities, there are a few iconic dishes and experiences that every visitor should try. From the creamy Clam Chowder to the delectable Lobster Rolls and the indulgent Boston Cream Pie, these dishes showcase the city's culinary heritage. Additionally, a visit to the Sam Adams Brewery for a tour is a must for beer enthusiasts. Here are some top restaurants in Boston where you can enjoy these local specialities:

Clam Chowder:

Legal Sea Foods

- Website: www.legalseafoods.com
- Contact: +1-617-266-7775
- Address: Second Floor @ Copley Place Mall, 100 Huntington Avenue, Boston, MA 02116
- Hours: Monday-Sunday: 11:00 AM - 10:00 PM

Legal Sea Foods is a renowned seafood restaurant that has been serving Boston's iconic Clam Chowder for over six decades. Made with fresh clams, potatoes, onions, and a rich creamy base, their Clam Chowder is a classic New

England dish that shouldn't be missed. Pair it with a warm bread roll for a truly comforting meal.

Lobster Rolls:

- Neptune Oyster
- Website: www.neptuneoyster.com
- Contact: +1-617-742-3474
- Address: 63 Salem Street, Boston, MA 02113
- Hours: Monday-Sunday: 11:30 AM - 9:30 PM

Neptune Oyster is a small but highly regarded seafood spot in the North End. Their Lobster Rolls are a favourite among locals and visitors alike. Served on a buttered and toasted roll, the lobster meat is tender and succulent, creating a truly satisfying bite. Be prepared for a wait, as the restaurant's popularity often results in a line.

Boston Cream Pie:

- Parker's Restaurant
- Website: www.omnihotels.com
- Contact: +1-617-227-8600
- Address: 60 School Street, Boston, MA 02108
- Hours: Monday-Sunday: 6:30 AM - 10:00 PM

Parker's Restaurant, located in the Omni Parker House Hotel, is famous for its Boston Cream Pie, a delectable dessert that originated in the city. This luscious treat features layers of sponge cake filled with vanilla custard and topped with chocolate ganache. Enjoy a slice of Boston's culinary history in an elegant and historic setting.

Sam Adams Brewery Tour:
Samuel Adams Boston Brewery

- Website:www.samueladams.com/brewery/boston
- Contact: +1-617-368-5080
- Address: 30 Germania Street, Boston, MA 02130
- Hours: Monday-Thursday: 11:00 AM - 6:00 PM
- Friday-Sunday: 10:00 AM - 6:00 PM
- Price Range: Free (Brewery Tours available for a fee)

To complete your Boston food experience, don't miss the opportunity to take a tour of the Samuel Adams Boston Brewery. Learn about the beer-making process, sample a variety of their brews, and discover the rich history of this iconic Boston brewery. Note that while the tours are usually free, certain speciality tours may have a fee.

Please note that restaurant hours and prices are subject to change, so it's always a good idea to check their websites or call ahead for the most up-to-date information.

CHAPTER 8

ACCOMMODATION OPTIONS

Luxury Hotels

With its rich history, cultural heritage, and vibrant atmosphere, Boston is home to a range of luxury hotels that cater to the discerning traveller. These hotels offer impeccable service, elegant accommodations, and top-notch amenities, ensuring a truly memorable stay. Allow me to introduce you to some of the top luxury hotels in Boston:

The Liberty, a Luxury Collection Hotel

- Website: www.libertyhotel.com

- Address: 215 Charles Street, Boston, MA 02114
- Contact: +1-617-224-4000
- Price per night: Starting from $350

Located in the historic Beacon Hill neighbourhood, The Liberty is a beautifully restored 19th-century jail-turned-luxury hotel. With its stunning architecture, stylish rooms, and a rooftop bar overlooking the city, this hotel provides a unique and luxurious experience for guests.

The Langham, Boston
- Website: www.langhamhotels.com/boston
- Address: 250 Franklin Street, Boston, MA 02110
- Contact: +1-617-451-1900
- Price per night: Starting from $400

Situated in the heart of downtown Boston, The Langham offers timeless elegance and impeccable service. With its luxurious rooms, an award-winning spa, and exquisite dining options, including the renowned Café Fleuri, this hotel provides a refined and indulgent experience.

Four Seasons Hotel Boston
- Website: www.fourseasons.com/boston

- Address: 200 Boylston Street, Boston, MA 02116
- Contact: +1-617-338-4400
- Price per night: Starting from $300

Overlooking the Boston Public Garden, the Four Seasons Hotel Boston combines classic charm with modern sophistication. Its spacious rooms, exceptional amenities, including a full-service spa and fitness centre, and renowned dining at The Bristol, make it a favourite among luxury travellers.

The Ritz-Carlton, Boston

- Website: www.ritzcarlton.com/boston
- Address: 10 Avery Street, Boston, MA 02111
- Contact: +1-617-574-7100
- Price per night: Starting from $250

Located in the bustling Midtown neighbourhood, The Ritz-Carlton offers luxurious accommodations and unparalleled service. With its opulent rooms, a rooftop terrace with panoramic city views, and a Michelin-starred restaurant, Artisan Bistro, this hotel provides a lavish and sophisticated experience.

Mandarin Oriental, Boston

- Website: www.mandarinoriental.com/boston
- Address: 776 Boylston Street, Boston, MA 02199
- Contact: +1-617-535-8888
- Price per night: Starting from $200

Situated in the upscale Back Bay neighbourhood, the Mandarin Oriental combines elegance with modern sophistication. Its luxurious rooms, award-winning spa, and fine dining at Bar Boulud make it a premier choice for luxury travellers seeking refined accommodations.

The Fairmont Copley Plaza

- Website:www.fairmont.com/copley-plaza-Boston
- Address: 138 St James Avenue, Boston, MA 02116
- Contact: +1-617-267-5300
- Price per night: Starting from $300

A historic landmark in the Back Bay area, The Fairmont Copley Plaza offers timeless elegance and exceptional service. With its grand lobby, luxurious rooms, and a rooftop health club, this hotel exudes luxury and provides a memorable stay.

For travellers seeking comfortable and affordable accommodations without compromising on quality, Boston offers a range of mid-range hotels that provide a pleasant stay at a reasonable price. These hotels combine convenience, comfort, and value, ensuring a satisfying experience for visitors. Here are some top mid-range hotels in Boston:

The Godfrey Hotel Boston

- Website: www.godfreyhotelboston.com
- Address: 505 Washington Street, Boston, MA 02111
- Contact: +1-617-804-2000
- Price per night: Starting from $150

Located in downtown Boston, The Godfrey Hotel offers contemporary design, stylish rooms, and modern amenities. With its prime location near popular attractions like Boston Common and the Theatre District, this hotel provides easy access to the city's vibrant energy.

Residence Inn by Marriott Boston Downtown/Seaport

- Website: www.marriott.com/bosrp
- Address: 370 Congress Street, Boston, MA 02210
- Contact: +1-617-478-0840
- Price per night: Starting from $180

Situated in the trendy Seaport District, the Residence Inn by Marriott offers spacious suites with fully equipped kitchens, making it ideal for extended stays. Guests can enjoy complimentary breakfast, a fitness centre, and a convenient location near the Boston Tea Party Ships & Museum.

Hampton Inn & Suites Boston Crosstown Center

- Website:www.hamptoninn3.hilton.com/boston-crosstown-center
- Address: 811 Massachusetts Avenue, Boston, MA 02118
- Contact: +1-617-445-6400
- Price per night: Starting from $130

Conveniently located near the Boston Medical Center and Northeastern University, the Hampton Inn & Suites offers comfortable rooms, a complimentary hot breakfast, and a fitness centre. Its proximity to public transportation allows for easy exploration of Boston's attractions.

Courtyard by Marriott Boston Downtown

- Website: www.marriott.com/bosdm
- Address: 275 Tremont Street, Boston, MA 02116
- Contact: +1-617-426-1400
- Price per night: Starting from $160

Situated in the vibrant Theatre District, the Courtyard by Marriott provides modern rooms, a fitness centre, and an on-site restaurant. Its central location offers easy access to popular landmarks like Boston Common and the Freedom Trail.

Hyatt Regency Boston

- Website:www.hyatt.com/en-US/hotel/massachusetts/hyatt-regency-Boston
- Address: 1 Avenue de Lafayette, Boston, MA 02111
- Contact: +1-617-912-1234

- Price per night: Starting from $170

Located near Boston's historic Chinatown and Theater District, the Hyatt Regency Boston features comfortable rooms, a fitness centre, and a rooftop terrace. Its proximity to public transportation allows for convenient exploration of the city.

Budget-Friendly Hotels

For travellers looking for affordable accommodations without sacrificing comfort and convenience, Boston offers a selection of budget-friendly hotels that provide a pleasant stay at wallet-friendly prices. These hotels offer value for money, ensuring a comfortable and enjoyable experience for visitors on a budget. Here are some top budget-friendly hotels in Boston:

HI Boston Hostel

- Website:www.hiusa.org/hostels/massachusetts/boston/boston
- Address: 19 Stuart Street, Boston, MA 02116
- Contact: +1-617-536-9455
- Price per night: Starting from $40 (dormitory-style rooms)

Located in the heart of downtown Boston, HI Boston Hostel offers affordable accommodations in a vibrant and social atmosphere. With shared dormitory-style rooms, a communal kitchen, and organized activities, this hostel is perfect for budget travellers looking to meet fellow adventurers.

Harborside Inn

- Website: www.harborsideinnboston.com
- Address: 185 State Street, Boston, MA 02109
- Contact: +1-617-723-7500
- Price per night: Starting from $100

Situated near Boston's waterfront and the historic Faneuil Hall Marketplace, the Harborside Inn offers cosy and affordable rooms with a touch of charm. Its central location allows for easy access to popular attractions and public transportation.

The Constitution Inn

- Website: www.constitutioninn.org
- Address: 150 Third Avenue, Boston, MA 02129
- Contact: +1-617-241-8400
- Price per night: Starting from $90

Located in the historic Charlestown Navy Yard, The Constitution Inn offers affordable accommodations with easy access to downtown Boston. With its fitness centre, indoor swimming pool, and proximity to the USS Constitution Museum, it provides a comfortable stay for budget-conscious travellers.

Midtown Hotel

- Website: www.midtownhotel.com
- Address: 220 Huntington Avenue, Boston, MA 02115
- Contact: +1-617-262-1000
- Price per night: Starting from $80

Situated near Boston's Symphony Hall and Fenway Park, the Midtown Hotel offers affordable rooms in a convenient location. With its friendly service and proximity to public transportation, it's an ideal choice for budget travellers exploring the city.

The Boston Common Hotel and Conference Center

- Website: www.bostoncommonhotel.com
- Address: 40 Trinity Place, Boston, MA 02116
- Contact: +1-617-933-7700
- Price per night: Starting from $70

Located near Boston Common and the Theater District, The Boston Common Hotel provides affordable accommodations with comfortable rooms and a friendly atmosphere. Its central location allows for easy access to popular attractions and public transportation.

Bed and Breakfasts

For travellers seeking a cosy and personalized accommodation experience, Boston offers a charming selection of bed and breakfasts that provide a warm and inviting atmosphere. These establishments combine comfortable lodging with a homely ambience and often include a delicious breakfast to start your day off right. Here are some top bed and breakfasts in Boston:

Aisling Bed and Breakfast
- Website: www.aisling-bostonbb.com
- Address: 21 E Broadway, South Boston, MA 02127
- Contact: +1-617-394-2848
- Price per night: Starting from $150

Located in the vibrant South Boston neighbourhood, Aisling Bed and Breakfast offers comfortable rooms with a touch of Irish hospitality. The cosy atmosphere, complimentary breakfast, and convenient access to local attractions make it an excellent choice for a relaxing stay.

Clarendon Square Bed and Breakfast

- Website: www.clarendonsquare.com
- Address: 198 West Brookline Street, Boston, MA 02118
- Contact: +1-617-536-2229
- Price per night: Starting from $200

Nestled in the South End neighbourhood, Clarendon Square Bed and Breakfast offers elegant rooms and a tranquil garden oasis. With its sophisticated decor, homemade breakfast, and proximity to restaurants and shops, it provides a charming retreat in the heart of the city.

Taylor House Bed and Breakfast

- Website: www.taylorhouse.com
- Address: 50 Burroughs Street, Boston, MA 02130
- Contact: +1-617-983-9334
- Price per night: Starting from $175

Situated in the Jamaica Plain neighbourhood, Taylor House Bed and Breakfast offers Victorian-style accommodations in a historic setting. The cosy rooms, hearty breakfast, and proximity to the Arnold Arboretum make it a delightful choice for nature lovers and history enthusiasts.

Gryphon House

- Website: www.gryphonhouse.com
- Address: 9 Bay State Road, Boston, MA 02215
- Contact: +1-617-375-9003
- Price per night: Starting from $175

Located near the Boston University campus, Gryphon House provides comfortable accommodations with a touch of whimsy. The unique decor, homemade breakfast, and convenient access to Fenway Park and the Charles River make it an ideal choice for sports enthusiasts and explorers.

Moroccan Luxury Suites

- Website: www.moroccanluxurysuites.com
- Address: 8 Salem Street, Boston, MA 02113
- Contact: +1-617-706-4046
- Price per night: Starting from $175

Situated in the historic North End neighbourhood, Moroccan Luxury Suites offers exotic and opulent accommodations inspired by Moroccan design. The luxurious rooms, warm hospitality, and proximity to authentic Italian restaurants make it a memorable choice for a unique and indulgent stay.

These bed and breakfasts in Boston provide a cosy and personalized alternative to traditional hotels, allowing you to experience the city with a touch of warmth and hospitality. Enjoy a comfortable stay, delicious breakfast, and the personalized attention of friendly hosts during your visit to Boston.

CHAPTER 9

ITINERARY IN BOSTON

One-week itinerary in Boston

Day 1: Beacon Hill Exploration

MORNING

- Start your trip in the historic Beacon Hill neighbourhood and explore the charming cobblestone streets and brownstones.
- Stop for breakfast at The Paramount, a local diner known for its pancakes and omelettes.

AFTERNOON

- Visit the nearby Boston Common, the city's oldest park, and take a swan boat ride in the Public Garden.
- Stop for lunch at Union Oyster House, a historic restaurant that's been serving seafood since 1826.

EVENING

- End your day with a visit to the famous Cheers bar, which inspired the TV show, and have a drink in the cosy basement bar.

Day 2: Salem Witch Trials and Art Appreciation

MORNING

- Take a day trip to Salem, a historic town known for its witch trials.
- Visit the Witch House, the only remaining building with direct ties to the trials, and explore the town's charming streets and shops.
- Stop for lunch at Turner's Seafood, a local favourite known for its seafood.

AFTERNOON

- Head back to Boston and visit the Museum of Fine Arts, which houses an impressive collection of artwork from around the world.
- Stop for dinner at Mistral, a French-inspired restaurant that's been voted the city's best.

EVENING

- End your day with a stroll through the trendy South End neighbourhood and stop for a drink at one of its many bars.

Day 3: Fenway Park and Presidential History

MORNING

- Start your day with a visit to the iconic Fenway Park, home of the Boston Red Sox.
- Take a tour of the stadium and visit the nearby Red Sox Hall of Fame.
- Stop for lunch at Tasty Burger, a local chain known for its delicious burgers and fries.

AFTERNOON

- Visit the John F. Kennedy Presidential Library and Museum, which showcases the life and legacy of the 35th president.
- Stop for dinner at Legal Sea Foods, a local seafood chain that's been serving fresh fish since 1950.

EVENING

- *End your day with a visit to the Top of the Hub, a restaurant and bar located on the 52nd floor of the Prudential Tower, for stunning views of the city skyline.*

Day 4: Harvard University and Cambridge

MORNING

- Take a day trip to the historic city of Cambridge and visit Harvard University, one of the country's oldest and most prestigious universities.
- Take a tour of the campus and visit the Harvard Art Museums.
- Stop for lunch at Craigie on Main, a restaurant known for its innovative American cuisine.

AFTERNOON

- Visit the nearby MIT Museum and learn about the history of science and technology.

- Stop for dinner at Oleana, a Mediterranean-inspired restaurant that's been named one of the country's best.

EVENING
- End your day with a visit to the Boston Tea Party Ships and Museum, which brings the famous event to life with interactive exhibits and live reenactments.

Day 5: USS Constitution and Bunker Hill

MORNING
- Start your day with a visit to the historic USS Constitution Museum, which tells the story of "Old Ironsides," the world's oldest commissioned warship afloat.
- Take a tour of the ship and watch the crew perform a cannon firing demonstration.
- Stop for lunch at Neptune Oyster, a small seafood restaurant known for its lobster rolls.

AFTERNOON

- Visit the nearby Bunker Hill Monument and climb the 294 steps to the top for panoramic views of the city.
- Stop for dinner at No. 9 Park, a fine dining restaurant that's been named the city's best.

EVENING

- End your day with a visit to the lively North End neighbourhood, also known as "Little Italy," and stop for a cannoli at Mike's Pastry.

Day 6: Concord Literary Tour and Revolutionary History

MORNING

- Take a day trip to the picturesque town of Concord and visit the homes of famous American authors Ralph Waldo Emerson and Louisa May Alcott.
- Stop for lunch at Woods Hill Table, a farm-to-table restaurant located on a nearby farm.

AFTERNOON

- Visit the nearby Minute Man National Historical Park and learn about the Revolutionary War battles that took place there.
- Stop for dinner at The Gallows, a gastropub known for its creative cocktails and burgers.

EVENING

- End your day with a visit to the historic Faneuil Hall Marketplace, a bustling indoor-outdoor shopping and dining destination that's been a fixture of the city since 1742.
- Note: Remember to find and book amazing hotels in Boston for each night to ensure a comfortable stay throughout your week-long itinerary.

CHAPTER 10

Cafés

A Blend of Flavors and Atmosphere

Boston boasts a vibrant cafe culture that caters to a diverse range of tastes and preferences. From cosy neighbourhood joints to chic and modern establishments, the city offers an array of cafes that are perfect for a relaxing break or a productive work session. Here are the top five cafes in Boston, each offering its unique charm and culinary delights.

Thinking Cup

- Address: 165 Tremont St, Boston, MA 02111
- How to get there: Thinking Cup is conveniently located in downtown Boston, just a short walk from the Park Street or Downtown Crossing T stations.

Known for its exceptional coffee and cosy ambience, Thinking Cup is a favourite among locals and visitors alike. The cafe takes pride in serving direct-trade coffee from around the world, prepared by skilled baristas. Pair your coffee with their delectable pastries and sandwiches made from locally sourced ingredients. With its rustic decor and friendly atmosphere, Thinking Cup is an ideal spot for a laid-back coffee experience.

Tatte Bakery & Cafe

- Address: Multiple locations in Boston, including 70 Charles St, Boston, MA 02114
- How to get there: Tatte Bakery & Cafe has several locations throughout Boston, including the picturesque Charles Street in Beacon Hill, easily accessible by public transportation or on foot.

Tatte Bakery & Cafe is renowned for its artisanal pastries, mouthwatering brunch options, and stylish interior design. The cafe's European-inspired atmosphere creates a warm and inviting space to enjoy their signature avocado tartine, shakshuka, or an assortment of freshly baked croissants. Tatte is the perfect choice for those seeking a blend of elegance and flavour in a cosy setting.

Render Coffee

- Address: 121 Devonshire St, Boston, MA 02109
- How to get there: Located in the Financial District, Render Coffee is conveniently accessible by public transportation, with the Downtown Crossing and Park Street T stations within walking distance.

With its minimalist decor and dedication to serving high-quality coffee, Render Coffee has become a popular destination for coffee enthusiasts. The cafe offers a variety of speciality brews prepared with precision and care. Enjoy the smooth flavours of their pour-over coffee or indulge in a rich espresso-based drink. Whether you're looking for a quick caffeine fix or a place to catch up with friends, Render Coffee offers a laid-back and welcoming environment.

Flour Bakery + Cafe

- Address: Multiple locations in Boston, including 12 Farnsworth St, Boston, MA 02210

- How to get there: Flour Bakery + Cafe has multiple locations in Boston, including the Fort Point neighbourhood, easily accessible by public transportation or a short walk from South Station.

Flour Bakery + Cafe is a beloved Boston institution known for its delectable pastries, sandwiches, and brunch options. Founded by James Beard Award-winning pastry chef Joanne Chang, the cafe delights visitors with its mouthwatering desserts, including the famous sticky buns and homemade Pop-Tarts. Enjoy a hearty sandwich or salad, paired with a perfectly brewed cup of coffee, amidst the cosy and bustling atmosphere of Flour Bakery + Cafe.

Pavement Coffeehouse

- Address: Multiple locations in Boston, including 286 Newbury St, Boston, MA 02115
- How to get there: Pavement Coffeehouse has multiple locations in Boston, including the iconic Newbury Street, easily accessible by public transportation or a short walk from Hynes Convention Center or Copley T stations.

Pavement Coffeehouse offers a hip and relaxed setting for coffee aficionados. With its industrial-chic decor, friendly staff, and ethically sourced coffee beans, Pavement creates a welcoming space for patrons. The cafe features an extensive menu of coffee options, including pour-overs, cold brews, and espresso-based drinks.

Bars and Pubs

Boston's vibrant nightlife scene is marked by its diverse array of bars and pubs, where locals and visitors gather to unwind, socialize, and enjoy a wide range of libations. From historic taverns to trendy craft beer bars, the city offers an exciting mix of establishments to suit every taste. Here are the top five bars and pubs in Boston, each offering its unique ambience and drinks.

Cheers

- Address: 84 Beacon St, Boston, MA 02108
- Hours: Monday-Sunday: 11:00 am - 2:00 am
- How to get there: Cheers is located in the Beacon Hill neighbourhood, easily accessible by public transportation. The nearest T station is Park Street, and the bar is a short walk from there.

Step into the iconic Cheers bar, the inspiration behind the famous TV show. This historic establishment captures the spirit of a traditional American pub, complete with wood-panelled walls and a cosy atmosphere. Enjoy a pint of local beer or indulge in a classic cocktail while immersing yourself in the nostalgia of the beloved sitcom. Cheer is a must-visit destination for fans of the show and those seeking a quintessential Boston bar experience.

The Burren

- Address: 247 Elm St, Somerville, MA 02144
- Hours: Monday-Friday: 11:30 am - 2:00 am; Saturday-Sunday: 10:30 am - 2:00 am
- How to get there: The Burren is located in Somerville, just north of Boston. Take the Red Line to Davis Square Station and enjoy a short walk to the pub.

Immerse yourself in Irish charm at The Burren, a lively pub known for its warm atmosphere and live music. This authentic Irish establishment offers a wide selection of Irish whiskies, beers, and traditional pub fare. Whether you're looking to enjoy a hearty meal, listen to traditional

Irish tunes, or engage in lively conversation, The Burren provides a genuine Irish pub experience right in the heart of Boston.

Trillium Brewing Company

- Address: 50 Thomson Pl, Boston, MA 02210
- Hours: Monday-Thursday: 12:00 pm - 10:00 pm; Friday-Saturday: 11:00 am - 11:00 pm; Sunday: 11:00 am - 9:00 pm
- How to get there: Trillium Brewing Company is located in the Fort Point neighbourhood. It's easily accessible by public transportation or a short walk from South Station.

Craft beer enthusiasts will delight in a visit to Trillium Brewing Company. This award-winning brewery showcases a rotating selection of meticulously crafted beers, including ales, lagers, and barrel-aged brews. The spacious taproom provides a welcoming atmosphere to sample their creations and learn about the brewing process. Trillium's commitment to quality and innovation has made it a staple in Boston's craft beer scene.

The Hawthorne

- Address: 500A Commonwealth Ave, Boston, MA 02215

- Hours: Monday-Saturday: 5:00 pm - 1:00 am; Sunday: 5:00 pm - 12:00 am

- How to get there: The Hawthorne is located in the Fenway-Kenmore neighbourhood, near Kenmore Square. It's easily accessible by public transportation, with Kenmore Station and Fenway Station within walking distance.

The Hawthorne is a sophisticated cocktail bar known for its innovative mixology and stylish ambience. The talented bartenders craft unique and artfully presented cocktails using fresh ingredients and creative techniques. The bar's elegant decor and intimate seating areas create an ideal setting for a memorable evening. Whether you're a cocktail connoisseur or simply looking to enjoy a well-crafted drink, The Hawthorne promises an exceptional experience.

Jacob Wirth

- Address: 31 Stuart St, Boston, MA 02116
- Hours: Monday-Saturday: 11:30 am - 12:00 am; Sunday: 12:00 pm - 12:00 am
- How to get there: Jacob Wirth is located in the Theater District, a short walk from Downtown Crossing and Park Street T stations.

Step back in time at Jacob Wirth, one of Boston's oldest German beer halls. This historic establishment has been serving Bavarian-inspired cuisine and an extensive beer selection since 1868. Enjoy a hearty German meal, such as sausages or schnitzel, while sipping on a stein of traditional German beer. The authentic atmosphere, complete with wooden booths and vintage decor, adds to the charm of this beloved Boston institution.

Unleash Your Nightlife Spirit in Boston

Boston's nightlife extends beyond bars and pubs, offering a vibrant scene for those seeking electrifying music, dancing, and unforgettable performances. From pulsating nightclubs to intimate live music venues, the city is home to a diverse array of establishments that cater to music lovers and partygoers alike. Here are the top five nightclubs and live music venues in Boston, each offering a unique experience for an exhilarating night out.

Royale

- Address: 279 Tremont St, Boston, MA 02116
- Hours: Friday-Saturday: 10:00 pm - 2:00 am
- How to get there: Royale is located in the Theater District, near Chinatown and Downtown Crossing. It's easily accessible by public transportation, with several T stations in the vicinity.

Step into the upscale world of Royale, a premier nightclub known for its impressive sound system, state-of-the-art lighting, and world-class DJs. This multi-level venue features a spacious dance floor, VIP areas, and an energetic atmosphere that keeps the party going until the early hours. From EDM to hip-hop, Royale offers a dynamic mix of music genres, ensuring an electrifying night of dancing and entertainment.

House of Blues

- Address: 15 Lansdowne St, Boston, MA 02215
- Hours: Varies depending on events
- How to get there: House of Blues is located near Fenway Park, in the lively Fenway-Kenmore neighbourhood. It's easily accessible by public transportation, with Kenmore Station and Fenway Station within walking distance.

Immerse yourself in the world of live music at House of Blues, a renowned venue that hosts a diverse range of performances, including concerts by local and international artists. This iconic establishment offers a spacious concert hall, multiple bars, and excellent acoustics to ensure an exceptional audio experience. Whether you're a fan of rock, blues, or pop, House of Blues delivers an unforgettable night of live music in an electric atmosphere.

The Sinclair

- Address: 52 Church St, Cambridge, MA 02138
- Hours: Varies depending on events
- How to get there: The Sinclair is located in Cambridge, just across the river from Boston. Take the Red Line to Harvard Square Station and enjoy a short walk to the venue.

Discover the intimate charm of The Sinclair, a popular live music venue that showcases both emerging and established artists across various genres. With its cosy atmosphere, excellent sound quality, and diverse lineup, this venue offers an up-close and personal experience with your favourite bands and musicians. Enjoy a night of live music in an intimate setting, and grab a drink at the bar to complement the vibrant performances.

Middle East Restaurant and Nightclub

- Address: 472-480 Massachusetts Ave, Cambridge, MA 02139

- Hours: Varies depending on events
- How to get there: The Middle East is located in Cambridge, near Central Square. Take the Red Line to Central Square Station and enjoy a short walk to the venue.

Dive into the eclectic music scene at the Middle East Restaurant and Nightclub, a cultural hub that hosts live performances ranging from indie rock to hip-hop and world music. With multiple stages, including a downstairs basement club, this venue offers an immersive experience for music enthusiasts. Enjoy live music, discover new artists, and savour delicious Middle Eastern cuisine in a laid-back and inclusive atmosphere.

Wally's Cafe Jazz Club

- Address: 427 Massachusetts Ave, Boston, MA 02118
- Hours: Monday-Sunday: 11:00 am - 2:00 am
- How to get there: Wally's Cafe is located in the South End neighbourhood, near Northeastern University. Take the Orange Line to Massachusetts Avenue Station and enjoy a short walk to the club.

Experience the soulful sounds of jazz at Wally's Cafe, a legendary jazz club that has been a staple of Boston's music scene since 1947. This intimate venue showcases talented local musicians, offering nightly live jazz performances that captivate the audience. With its cosy ambience and relaxed atmosphere, Wally's Cafe provides an authentic jazz club experience where you can unwind, enjoy fantastic music, and soak up the rich history of Boston's jazz culture

Boston's shopping scene offers a delightful mix of high-end boutiques, bustling marketplaces, and expansive shopping centres. From the fashionable Newbury Street boutiques to the historic Faneuil Hall Marketplace, the city provides a variety of shopping experiences to suit every taste and style. This guide will highlight the top shopping destinations in Boston, including Newbury Street Boutiques, Faneuil Hall Marketplace, Prudential Center Shops, and Cambridge Side Galleria. Additionally, we'll provide practical tips to enhance your shopping adventure in the city.

Newbury Street Boutiques:

Located in the upscale Back Bay neighbourhood, Newbury Street is a shopper's paradise lined with elegant brownstones and renowned boutiques. Stroll along this picturesque street and explore a wide range of designer stores, fashion boutiques, art galleries, and speciality shops. From international luxury brands to unique local designers, Newbury Street offers an unparalleled shopping experience for fashion enthusiasts.

Faneuil Hall Marketplace:

Located in the heart of downtown Boston, Faneuil Hall Marketplace is a historic shopping destination that combines retail, dining, and entertainment. Discover a vibrant mix of locally-owned shops, well-known brands, and artisanal market stalls. Don't miss Quincy Market, where you can savour delicious food from various vendors while browsing through an assortment of gift shops, boutiques, and speciality stores.

Prudential Center Shops:

Situated in the Back Bay neighbourhood, the Prudential Center is a premier shopping destination featuring a diverse selection of shops and boutiques. Explore designer brands, luxury retailers, department stores, and speciality shops, all conveniently located under one roof. The Prudential Center also offers stunning views of the city skyline from its Skywalk Observatory, making it a must-visit spot for both shopping and sightseeing.

Cambridge Side Galleria:

Cross the river to Cambridge and visit the Cambridge Side Galleria, a spacious shopping mall located near Kendall Square. This mall houses a wide range of stores, including popular fashion brands, electronics retailers, home goods, and beauty products. With its convenient location and ample parking, Cambridge Side Galleria provides a convenient shopping experience for visitors staying in Cambridge or exploring the nearby attractions.

Practical Tips for Shopping in Boston:

- Sales Tax: Keep in mind that Massachusetts has a sales tax of 6.25% on most retail purchases. Factor this into your budget when shopping.

- Store Hours: Most stores in Boston are open from Monday to Saturday, with Sunday hours varying. Larger shopping centres tend to have extended hours. Check individual store websites or contact them directly for their specific operating hours.

- Public Transportation: Boston's public transportation system, known as the MBTA or "T," is an efficient way to navigate the city. Many shopping areas are conveniently located near T stations, allowing for easy access without the need for parking.

- Dress Comfortably: Shopping in Boston often involves walking, so wear comfortable shoes and dress in layers, especially during colder months. Be prepared for New England's unpredictable weather.

- Souvenirs and Local Products: Look for authentic Boston souvenirs and locally-made products, such as handmade crafts and food items. Faneuil Hall

Marketplace and other market stalls are excellent places to find unique Boston-themed gifts.

- Bargaining: Bargaining is not common in most retail stores in Boston. However, you may find opportunities for negotiation at antique shops, flea markets, or street vendors.

Practical Tips and Safety

Currency: The official currency in Boston is the United States Dollar (USD). It is recommended to have some cash on hand for small purchases, as cash is widely accepted in the city.

Language: The official language in Boston is English. You'll find that English is spoken and understood throughout the city, including in hotels, restaurants, shops, and tourist areas.

Visa: Depending on your nationality, you may require a visa to enter the United States. It is important to check the visa requirements for your country well in advance of your trip. For most tourists, a valid passport is required for entry.

Money: Boston is a moderately expensive city, so it's a good idea to plan your budget accordingly. Credit cards are widely accepted in most establishments, but it is recommended to carry some cash for smaller purchases and in case of any unforeseen circumstances. Currency exchange services are available at banks, airports, and some hotels.

Mobile Phones: If you plan to use your mobile phone in Boston, ensure that you have an appropriate plan with your service provider to avoid high roaming charges. Most major mobile carriers offer coverage in the city, but be sure to check with your provider regarding international roaming rates.

Opening Hours: Here are some general opening hour guidelines for various establishments in Boston:

- Banks: Banks in Boston typically operate from Monday to Friday, with opening hours ranging from 9:00 AM to 5:00 PM. Some banks may have limited hours on Saturdays or offer extended hours on certain weekdays.
- Cafes and Bars: Cafes and bars in Boston have varied opening hours, but they generally open early in the morning and close late at night. Some

establishments may have limited hours on Sundays, so it's best to check their schedules.

- Museums: Museums in Boston are usually open from Tuesday to Sunday, with operating hours typically between 10:00 AM and 5:00 PM. Some museums may have extended hours on certain days or during the summer season.

- Restaurants: Restaurants in Boston serve lunch and dinner. Lunch hours usually start around 11:30 AM or noon and continue until 2:00 PM or 3:00 PM. Dinner service typically begins around 5:00 PM or 6:00 PM and extends until 9:00 PM or later, especially on weekends. It's advisable to make reservations for popular dining spots.

- Shops and Supermarkets: Most shops and supermarkets in Boston are open seven days a week. Weekday opening hours are generally from 9:00 AM to 6:00 PM or 7:00 PM. On Saturdays, shops usually close around 5:00 PM or 6:00 PM, while supermarkets may have extended hours, staying open until 8:00 PM or 9:00 PM.

Internet Access: Boston offers excellent internet connectivity, and most hotels, cafes, and restaurants provide free Wi-Fi for their customers. Additionally, you can find internet kiosks in public areas and libraries throughout the city. If you need constant internet access, consider purchasing a local SIM card with a data plan or using a portable Wi-Fi device.

Electricity: The standard voltage in Boston, as well as in the United States, is 120 volts, and the frequency is 60 Hz. The power outlets in Boston generally accept two- or three-pin plugs, so it's advisable to bring suitable adapters if your devices use different plug types.

Time Zone: Boston follows Eastern Standard Time (EST) during the standard time, and Eastern Daylight Time (EDT) during daylight saving time. The city is typically in the UTC-5 time zone during standard time and UTC-4 during daylight saving time.

Local Customs:

- Bostonians are known for their friendly and helpful nature. It is common courtesy to greet people with a smile and a simple "hello" or "good morning."

- When dining in a restaurant or attending a social event, it is customary to wait for the host to initiate the start of the meal or event.

- Bostonians take pride in their sports teams, particularly the Boston Red Sox (baseball), New England Patriots (football), Boston Celtics (basketball), and Boston Bruins (hockey). Engaging in friendly conversations about sports can be a great way to connect with locals.

Tipping Etiquette:

- Tipping is a customary practice in Boston, and it is expected to leave a gratuity for various services.

- In restaurants, it is customary to tip around 15-20% of the total bill before tax. Some restaurants may automatically add a gratuity for larger groups, so check your bill before adding tip.

- Bartenders usually receive a tip of $1-2 per drink, or 15-20% of the total bill if you have a tab.
- Taxi drivers and rideshare drivers appreciate a 10-15% tip of the total fare.
- It is customary to tip hotel staff who provide services such as valet parking, luggage assistance, and housekeeping. The typical tip amount is $2-5 per service.
- Other service providers, such as tour guides, hairdressers, and spa staff, also appreciate a tip of 15-20% of the service cost.

Emergency Contact Numbers:
- In case of an emergency, dial 911 from any phone in Boston. This number connects you to police, fire, and medical services.
- Non-emergency police assistance can be reached at 311 or the local police precinct.
- For medical advice or assistance, you can call the Massachusetts Poison Control Center at 1-800-222-1222.

- If you need consular assistance from your home country, contact your country's embassy or consulate in Boston.

Choosing the best time to visit Boston depends on various factors, including weather preferences, special events, and budget considerations.

Weather Considerations:

Summer (June to August): Summer is the most popular time to visit Boston, with warm temperatures averaging between 20°C and 30°C (68°F and 86°F). It's the perfect time to explore the city's outdoor attractions, enjoy the beautiful Boston Harbor, and attend outdoor festivals and concerts. However, be prepared for larger crowds and higher hotel prices during this peak tourist season.

Spring (March to May) and Autumn (September to November): Spring and autumn offer mild and pleasant temperatures ranging from 10°C to 20°C (50°F to 68°F). These seasons showcase the city's charming beauty, with blooming flowers in spring and vibrant fall foliage in autumn. It's a great time to explore historic sites, walk along the Freedom Trail, and enjoy outdoor activities without the summer crowds.

Winter (December to February): Winter in Boston is cold, with temperatures ranging from -3°C to 7°C (26°F to 45°F). However, if you enjoy winter activities and festive atmospheres, this can be a magical time to visit. Boston hosts seasonal events like ice skating on the Boston Common, the Boston Winter Holiday Market, and the First Night celebrations on New Year's Eve. Just remember to pack warm clothing and be prepared for occasional snowstorms.

Special Events:

Boston is a city that celebrates its rich culture and history through various festivals and events throughout the year. Here are some notable events to consider:

Boston Marathon (April): The Boston Marathon is one of the world's most prestigious and iconic races. If you're a sports enthusiast or want to witness the city's vibrant energy, visiting during the marathon is a thrilling experience.

Fourth of July (July): Boston's Fourth of July celebrations are legendary, featuring fireworks over the Charles River and numerous events commemorating Independence Day. It's an ideal time to experience patriotic fervour and enjoy outdoor concerts and festivities.

Boston Calling Music Festival (May): Music lovers should plan their visit during the Boston Calling Music Festival, which showcases a diverse lineup of local and international artists across different genres.

Head of the Charles Regatta (October): This renowned rowing event attracts competitors from around the world. Watching the races along the Charles River or enjoying the festive atmosphere from the riverbanks is a fantastic way to experience Boston's sporting culture.

Budget Considerations:

Boston is known for its vibrant urban atmosphere, but it's essential to consider budget considerations. Accommodation prices and tourist crowds tend to be higher during the summer months. To make the most of your budget, consider visiting during the shoulder seasons of spring and autumn when hotel rates are more affordable, and attractions are less crowded.

CHAPTER 11

RESOURCES & REFERENCES

Recommended Books and Films

As you embark on your journey to explore the historic and culturally rich city of Boston, why not delve deeper into its stories and immerse yourself in its fascinating narratives? Whether you're a bookworm seeking literary inspiration or a film enthusiast yearning for captivating visuals, here are some recommended books and films that will enhance your Boston experience and offer a glimpse into the city's unique charm.

Books:

"A Short History of Boston" by Robert J. Allison: Gain a comprehensive understanding of Boston's captivating history through this concise yet informative book. From its early colonial roots to the birth of the American Revolution and beyond, Allison provides an engaging narrative that brings the city's past to life.

"The Bostonians" by Henry James: Set in 19th-century Boston, this novel delves into the complexities of the city's social and cultural landscape. James skillfully explores themes of feminism, politics, and love, offering a nuanced perspective on the Boston society of that era.

"Make Way for Ducklings" by Robert McCloskey: A beloved children's book, "Make Way for Ducklings" takes readers on an endearing adventure through the iconic Boston Public Garden. Follow the journey of Mr and Mrs Mallard as they search for the perfect place to raise their ducklings in the heart of Boston.

"The Given Day" by Dennis Lehane: Set during the tumultuous era of the early 20th century, this historical novel intertwines the lives of working-class families, corrupt police officers, and emerging labour unions in Boston. Lehane's vivid storytelling captures the essence of the city's social dynamics during a transformative period.

"Mystic River" by Dennis Lehane: Dive into the gritty underbelly of Boston's neighbourhoods with this gripping crime novel. "Mystic River" explores the lives of three childhood friends whose paths diverge and intersect after a tragic event reshapes their lives. Lehane's masterful storytelling paints a vivid portrait of Boston's working-class communities.

Films:

"Good Will Hunting" (1997): This critically acclaimed film showcases the talents of actors Matt Damon and Ben Affleck, who also wrote the screenplay. Set against the backdrop of Cambridge, just across the Charles River from Boston, the movie tells the story of a young genius grappling with his identity and potential. It offers a glimpse into Boston's academic atmosphere and the city's working-class neighbourhoods.

"The Departed" (2006): Directed by Martin Scorsese, this crime drama is set in the gritty streets of Boston and features an all-star cast including Leonardo DiCaprio, Matt Damon, and Jack Nicholson. With its gripping plot and intense performances, the film delves into the interconnected worlds of the Boston Police Department and organized crime, offering a riveting portrayal of the city's darker side.

"Spotlight" (2015): Winner of the Academy Award for Best Picture, "Spotlight" sheds light on the investigative journalism of The Boston Globe's "Spotlight" team. The film follows their groundbreaking reporting on the widespread child abuse scandal within the Catholic Church. Through its compelling storytelling, "Spotlight" captures the resilience and determination of Boston's journalistic community.

"The Social Network" (2010): Although primarily set in Silicon Valley, this film delves into the early days of Facebook and its Harvard origins. Directed by David Fincher, it provides a glimpse into the innovative and entrepreneurial spirit that thrives in Boston's academic institutions.

"Fever Pitch" (2005): For a lighthearted romantic comedy with a Boston twist, "Fever Pitch" is the perfect choice. Starring Drew Barrymore and Jimmy Fallon, the film revolves around the passionate love affair between a Red Sox fanatic and a career-oriented woman. With the backdrop of Fenway Park and the energy of Boston's sports culture, this movie captures the city's deep connection to its beloved baseball team.

These recommended books and films offer a multifaceted perspective on Boston's history, culture, and unique character. Whether you're strolling along the cobblestone streets of Beacon Hill or exploring the vibrant neighbourhoods of Cambridge.

Helpful Websites, Apps, and Online Resources

Planning a trip to Boston can be an exciting adventure, but it's always helpful to have access to reliable and convenient online resources to make your travel experience smoother and more enjoyable. From budgeting apps to transportation websites, restaurant guides, and hotel booking platforms, here are some recommended online resources to assist you in navigating your way through the vibrant city of Boston.

Travel Budget Apps:

Mint: Mint is a popular budgeting app that allows you to track your expenses, create budgets, and manage your finances effectively. It provides a comprehensive overview of your spending habits, helping you stay on track with your travel budget and make informed financial decisions while exploring Boston.

Trail Wallet: Specifically designed for travellers, Trail Wallet helps you keep track of your expenses in different currencies. With its intuitive interface and convenient features, you can easily log your expenses, set daily or trip budgets, and receive visual insights into your spending patterns. This app is an excellent tool to manage your travel budget while exploring the diverse attractions of Boston.

Official Tourism Websites:

The Greater Boston Convention & Visitors Bureau (www.bostonusa.com): This official tourism website offers a wealth of information about Boston's attractions, events, dining, shopping, and accommodations. It provides comprehensive guides, interactive maps, and insider tips to help you plan your itinerary and discover the city's hidden gems.

Discover New England (www.discovernewengland.org): As part of the larger New England region, Boston is a gateway to exploring the charming towns and natural beauty of the area. The Discover New England website offers insights into the broader region, including travel itineraries, outdoor activities, and cultural experiences beyond the city limits.

Transportation Websites:

Massachusetts Bay Transportation Authority (MBTA) (www.mbta.com): The MBTA website and its official app, known as "MBTA mTicket," provide schedules, maps, and real-time updates for the city's subway (T), buses, and commuter trains. You can plan your routes, check fares, and receive service notifications to navigate Boston's public transportation system efficiently.

Uber and Lyft: Ride-hailing services like Uber and Lyft are widely available in Boston. Their respective websites or mobile apps allow you to request rides, estimate fares, and track your driver's location in real time. These services provide a convenient and reliable transportation option, particularly for getting around the city during late hours or when you prefer a door-to-door service.

Restaurant Websites:

Eater Boston (boston.eater.com): Eater Boston is a go-to resource for food enthusiasts, offering restaurant recommendations, news, and reviews. The website covers a wide range of cuisines, from casual eateries to fine dining establishments, ensuring you'll find something to satisfy your palate while in Boston.

Boston Magazine's Best Restaurants (www.bostonmagazine.com/best-restaurants): Boston Magazine's annual "Best Restaurants" list highlights the city's culinary scene, showcasing top-rated dining establishments across different categories. It's a great resource for discovering acclaimed restaurants and exploring Boston's vibrant food culture.

Yelp (www.yelp.com): Yelp is a popular online platform that provides user-generated reviews and ratings for restaurants in Boston. It offers a comprehensive database of dining establishments, allowing you to explore a variety of cuisines, read reviews, view menus, and find the perfect spot for a delicious meal. You can search by location, price range, and dietary preferences to discover culinary gems in Boston.

OpenTable (www.opentable.com): If you prefer making restaurant reservations in advance, OpenTable is a convenient website that allows you to book tables at numerous restaurants in Boston. With its user-friendly interface, you can search for available reservation times, read reviews, and secure your dining arrangements hassle-free.

Hotels Websites:

Expedia (www.expedia.com): Expedia is another popular online travel agency that allows you to compare prices and book hotels in Boston. The platform offers a wide range of options, from boutique hotels to major chains, along with customer reviews and convenient booking features.

Booking.com: Booking.com is a well-established hotel booking platform that offers a wide range of accommodation options in Boston. With its extensive database, you can search for hotels, compare prices, read guest reviews, and make reservations according to your preferences and budget. The website also provides detailed information on hotel amenities, location, and proximity to popular attractions.

TripAdvisor (www.tripadvisor.com): TripAdvisor is a comprehensive travel platform that includes hotel listings, reviews, and recommendations from fellow travellers. It offers an extensive collection of Boston hotels, allowing you to explore options based on user ratings, prices, and location. The website's interactive features help you make informed decisions and choose accommodations that best suit your needs.

CONCLUSIONS

As you come to the end of this Boston travel guidebook, we hope that it has provided you with valuable insights and useful information to make the most of your visit to this historic and vibrant city. Boston is a city rich in history, culture, and diverse experiences, and we have aimed to capture its essence and present it to you in an informative and engaging manner.

From the famous Freedom Trail, taking you on a journey through the city's revolutionary past, to the modern and bustling neighbourhoods like Back Bay and Beacon Hill, Boston offers a blend of old-world charm and contemporary energy. You have discovered iconic landmarks, such as the USS Constitution, Fenway Park, and the Boston Common, as well as hidden gems tucked away in the city's cobblestone streets.

We have guided you through Boston's culinary scene, showcasing its diverse gastronomic offerings, from mouthwatering seafood to international cuisines. Whether you're indulging in traditional clam chowder or exploring the vibrant food trucks, Boston promises to satisfy every food lover's palate.

Our guidebook has provided practical tips on transportation, shopping, and entertainment, equipping you with the knowledge to navigate the city with ease. From the efficient public transportation system to the charming boutiques along Newbury Street, you are well-prepared to embark on your Boston adventure.

We have also shared recommendations for top attractions, museums, parks, and cultural events, ensuring that you won't miss out on any of the city's must-see and must-do experiences. Whether you're immersing yourself in the rich history at the Museum of Fine Arts, catching a performance at the iconic Boston Symphony Orchestra, or exploring the vibrant street art scene, Boston offers a diverse range of activities to suit every interest.

As you explore Boston's neighbourhoods, you will discover the warmth and friendliness of its residents, who take pride in their city and are always willing to offer assistance or share their local knowledge. Embrace the Bostonian spirit and engage with the local community to truly immerse yourself in the city's unique atmosphere.

Remember to refer back to this guidebook whenever you need information or inspiration during your stay in Boston. And don't forget to explore the nearby attractions of New England, where charming towns, picturesque landscapes, and outdoor adventures await.

We hope that this guidebook has provided you with a comprehensive overview of Boston, from its historical significance to its vibrant present. May your journey in Boston be filled with unforgettable experiences, cherished memories, and a deep appreciation for this remarkable city. Safe travels, and enjoy your time in Boston!

Dear Reader:

Thank you for taking the time to read my book. I hope it provided you with some enlightenment, entertainment, or both. If you enjoyed it, I would be most grateful if you could leave a review on Amazon. Reviews are invaluable to authors, as they help spread the word about the book and give potential readers an idea of what to expect.

Your honest opinion, even if it's not glowing, would be greatly appreciated and immensely helpful.

Thank you for your consideration.